BIBLE WISDOM FOR New Parents

COMPILED BY GARY WILDE

Christian
Parenting
B O O K S

Christian Parenting Books is an imprint of Chariot Family Publishing, a division of David C. Cook Publishing Co., Elgin, Illinois 60120 David C. Cook Publishing Co., Weston, Ontario Nova Distribution Ltd., Newton Abbot, England

Christian Parenting Today Magazine P.O. Box 850, Sisters, OR 97759 (800) 238-2221

BIBLE WISDOM FOR NEW PARENTS ©1993 by Chariot Family Publishing

Cover design by Foster Design Associates Interior Design by Glass House Graphics Compiled by Gary Wilde

First Printing, 1993   ISBN 0-78140-149-6 Printed in the United States of America 97 96 95 94 93 5 4 3 2 1

===TABLE OF CONTENTS===

═══ CHAPTER 1 ═══

'How can I express my gratitude to God for this wonderful gift—our newborn child?'

There I was, standing in the newborn nursery, looking down at my infant son," said Phillip. "I was overwhelmed with the miracle laying in that little crib. I remember pointing and talking to anybody who'd stop and listen: 'Look at those tiny fingers and toes; see his cute little smile; what a head of hair!' My little boy seemed to be resting so peacefully, a perfect creation of our great Creator.

"I was so overjoyed with God's goodness. I wanted to lift up my hands in praise, the way they used to do it in the Old Testament. Snatches of the Psalms kept running through my mind. As soon as I got home that night, I went to my Bible and read my favorite praise passages, my heart filled with worship. I can't think of a more wonderful day in my life."

FOR MEMORY:

The Mighty One has done great things for me—holy is his name.

Luke 1:49

FOR SILENT REFLECTION:

- *Do I view my children as gifts from God?*

- *How have I shown my gratitude to God for allowing me to become a parent?*

- *What will it mean for me to "delight in" this child in the years ahead?*

- *What aspects of childlikeness would I like to build into my adult life in the coming years?*

Sing and Shout for Joy!

I will praise you, O LORD, with all my heart;
I will tell of all your wonders.
I will be glad and rejoice in you;
I will sing praise to your name,
O Most High.
My enemies turn back;
they stumble and perish before you.
For you have upheld my right and my cause;
you have sat on your throne,
judging righteously.
You have rebuked the nations
and destroyed the wicked;
you have blotted out their name
for ever and ever.

Psalm 9:1-5

Shout with joy to God, all the earth!
Sing the glory of his name;
make his praise glorious!
Say to God, "How awesome are your deeds!
So great is your power
that your enemies cringe before you.
All the earth bows down to you;
they sing praise to you,
they sing praise to your name."

Psalm 66:1-4

13

Come, let us sing for joy to the LORD;
let us shout aloud to the Rock of our salvation.
Let us come before him with thanksgiving
and extol him with music and song.
For the LORD is the great God,
the great King above all gods.
In his hand are the depths of the earth,
and the mountain peaks belong to him.
The sea is his, for he made it,
and his hands formed the dry land.
Come, let us bow down in worship,
let us kneel before the LORD our Maker;
for he is our God
and we are the people of his pasture,
the flock under his care.

Psalm 95:1-7a

Praise him with the sounding of the trumpet,
praise him with the harp and lyre,
praise him with tambourine and dancing,
praise him with the strings and flute,
praise him with the clash of cymbals,
praise him with resounding cymbals.
Let everything that has breath praise the LORD.
Praise the LORD.

Psalm 150:3-6

14

Be Thankful: God Has Blessed You!

Sons are a heritage from the LORD,
children a reward from him.

Psalm 127:3

Our mouths were filled with laughter,
our tongues with songs of joy.
Then it was said among the nations,
"The LORD has done great things for them."

Psalm 126:2

He will yet fill your mouth with laughter
and your lips with shouts of joy.

Job 8:21

For Life Itself

Then God said, "Let the land produce vegetation: seedbearing plants and trees on the land that bear fruit with seed in it, according to their various kinds." And it was so. The land produced vegetation: plants bearing seed according to their kinds and trees bearing fruit with seed in it according to their kinds. And God saw that it was good. And there was evening, and there was morning—the third day.

And God said, "Let there be lights in the expanse of the sky to separate the day from the night, and let them serve as signs to mark seasons and days and years, and let them be lights in the expanse of the sky to give light on the earth." And it was so. God made two great lights—the greater light to govern the day and the lesser light to govern the night. He also made the stars. God set them in the expanse of the sky to give light on the earth, to govern the day and the night, and to separate light from darkness. And God saw that it was good. And there was evening, and there was morning—the fourth day.

And God said, "Let the water teem with living creatures, and let birds fly above the earth across the expanse of the sky." So God created the great creatures of the sea and every living and moving thing with which the water teems, according to their kinds, and every winged bird according to its kind. And God saw that it was good. God blessed them and said, "Be fruitful and increase in number and fill the water in the seas, and let the birds increase on the earth." And there was evening, and there was morning—the fifth day.

And God said, "Let the land produce living creatures according to their kinds: livestock, creatures that move along the ground, and wild animals, each according to its kind." And it was so. God made the wild animals according to their kinds, the livestock according to their kinds, and all the creatures that move along the ground according to their kinds. And God saw that it was good.

Then God said, "Let us make man in our image, in our likeness, and let them rule over the fish of the sea and the birds of the air, over the livestock, over all the earth, and over all the creatures that move along the ground." So God created man in his own image, in the image of God he created him; male and female he created them. God blessed them and said to them, "Be fruitful and increase in number; fill the earth and subdue it. Rule over the fish of the sea and the birds of the air and over every living creature that moves on the ground."

Then God said, "I give you every seedbearing plant on the face of the whole earth and every tree that has fruit with seed in it. They will be yours for food. And to all the beasts of the earth and all the birds of the air and all the creatures that move on the ground—everything that has the breath of life in it—I give every green plant for food." And it was so.

Genesis 1:11-30

For Salvation

He lifted me out of the slimy pit,
out of the mud and mire;
he set my feet on a rock
and gave me a firm place to stand.
He put a new song in my mouth,
a hymn of praise to our God.
Many will see and fear

17

and put their trust in the LORD.
Blessed is the man
who makes the LORD his trust,
who does not look to the proud,
to those who turn aside to false gods.
Many, O LORD my God,
are the wonders you have done.
The things you planned for us
no one can recount to you;
were I to speak and tell of them,
they would be too many to declare.

Psalm 40:2-5

Praise be to the God and Father of our Lord Jesus
Christ, who has blessed us in the heavenly realms
with every spiritual blessing in Christ. For he chose
us in him before the creation of the world to be holy
and blameless in his sight. In love he predestined us
to be adopted as his sons through Jesus Christ, in
accordance with his pleasure and will—to the praise
of his glorious grace, which he has freely given us in
the One he loves. In him we have redemption
through his blood, the forgiveness of sins, in accordance with the riches of God's grace that he lavished
on us with all wisdom and understanding. And he
made known to us the mystery of his will according
to his good pleasure, which he purposed in Christ, to
be put into effect when the times will have reached

their fulfillment—to bring all things in heaven and on earth together under one head, even Christ.

In him we were also chosen, having been predestined according to the plan of him who works out everything in conformity with the purpose of his will, in order that we, who were the first to hope in Christ, might be for the praise of his glory.

Ephesians 1:3-12

Giving thanks to the Father, who has qualified you to share in the inheritance of the saints in the kingdom of light.

Colossians 1:12

For God's Love and Care

The LORD is my shepherd,
I shall not be in want.
He makes me lie down in green pastures,
he leads me beside quiet waters,
he restores my soul.
He guides me in paths of righteousness
for his name's sake.
Even though I walk through the valley of the shadow of death,
I will fear no evil, for you are with me;
your rod and your staff, they comfort me.
You prepare a table before me in the presence of my enemies.

19

You anoint my head with oil;
my cup overflows.
Surely goodness and love will follow me
all the days of my life,
and I will dwell in the house of the LORD forever.

Psalm 23:1-6

It is good to praise the LORD
and make music to your name, O Most High,
to proclaim your love in the morning
and your faithfulness at night,
to the music of the ten-stringed lyre
and the melody of the harp.
For you make me glad by your deeds,
O LORD; I sing for joy at the works of your hands.

Psalm 92:1-4

I will tell of the kindnesses of the LORD,
the deeds for which he is to be praised,
according to all the LORD has done for us—
yes, the many good things he has done for the house
of Israel,
according to his compassion and many kindnesses.

Isaiah 63:7

And we know that in all things God works for the good
of those who love him, who have been called according
to his purpose. . . . If God is for us, who can be against

us? He who did not spare his own Son, but gave him up for us all—how will he not also, along with him, graciously give us all things? . . . Who shall separate us from the love of Christ? Shall trouble or hardship or persecution or famine or nakedness or danger or sword? . . .

No, in all these things we are more than conquerors through him who loved us. For I am convinced that neither death nor life, neither angels nor demons, neither the present nor the future, nor any powers, neither height nor depth, nor anything else in all creation, will be able to separate us from the love of God that is in Christ Jesus our Lord.

Romans 8:28-39

Delight in Children, as God Does

This is what the LORD says:
"I will return to Zion and dwell in Jerusalem.
Then Jerusalem will be called the City of Truth,
and the mountain of the LORD Almighty
will be called the Holy Mountain."
This is what the LORD Almighty says:
"Once again men and women of ripe old age
will sit in the streets of Jerusalem,
each with cane in hand because of his age.
The city streets will be filled
with boys and girls playing there."

Zechariah 8:3-5

Jesus Was a Pleasing Son

The Spirit of the LORD will rest on him—
the Spirit of wisdom and of understanding,
the Spirit of counsel and of power,
the Spirit of knowledge and of the fear of the
LORD—
and he will delight in the fear of the LORD.
He will not judge by what he sees with his eyes,
or decide by what he hears with his ears;
but with righteousness he will judge the needy,
with justice he will give decisions for the poor of the
earth.
He will strike the earth with the rod of his mouth;
with the breath of his lips he will slay the wicked.
Righteousness will be his belt
and faithfulness the sash around his waist.

Isaiah 11:2-5

When Elizabeth heard Mary's greeting, the baby
leaped in her womb, and Elizabeth was filled with
the Holy Spirit. In a loud voice she exclaimed:
"Blessed are you among women, and blessed is the
child you will bear!" . . .

And Mary said: "My soul glorifies the Lord
and my spirit rejoices in God my Savior,
for he has been mindful of the humble state of his
servant.

From now on all generations will call me blessed,
for the Mighty One has done great things for me—
holy is his name.
His mercy extends to those who fear him,
from generation to generation.
He has performed mighty deeds with his arm;
he has scattered those who are proud in their inmost
thoughts.
He has brought down rulers from their thrones
but has lifted up the humble.
He has filled the hungry with good things
but has sent the rich away empty.
He has helped his servant Israel,
remembering to be merciful
to Abraham and his descendants forever,
even as he said to our fathers."

Luke 1:41, 46-55

After six days Jesus took with him Peter, James and
John the brother of James, and led them up a high
mountain by themselves. There he was transfigured
before them. His face shone like the sun, and his
clothes became as white as the light. Just then there
appeared before them Moses and Elijah, talking with
Jesus.

Peter said to Jesus, "Lord, it is good for us to be
here. If you wish, I will put up three shelters—one
for you, one for Moses and one for Elijah."

23

While he was still speaking, a bright cloud
enveloped them, and a voice from the cloud said,
"This is my Son, whom I love; with him I am well
pleased. Listen to him!"

Matthew 17:1-5

And Jesus grew in wisdom and stature, and in favor
with God and men.

Luke 2:52

You Are a Child of Spiritual Birth

How great is the love the Father has lavished on us,
that we should be called children of God! And that is
what we are! The reason the world does not know
us is that it did not know him.

Dear friends, now we are children of God, and
what we will be has not yet been made known. But
we know that when he appears, we shall be like
him, for we shall see him as he is. Everyone who has
this hope in him purifies himself, just as he is pure.
Everyone who sins breaks the law; in fact, sin is law-
lessness. But you know that he appeared so that he
might take away our sins. And in him is no sin. No
one who lives in him keeps on sinning. No one who
continues to sin has either seen him or known him.

Dear children, do not let anyone lead you astray.
He who does what is right is righteous, just as he is
righteous. He who does what is sinful is of the devil,

because the devil has been sinning from the beginning. The reason the Son of God appeared was to destroy the devil's work. No one who is born of God will continue to sin, because God's seed remains in him; he cannot go on sinning, because he has been born of God. This is how we know who the children of God are and who the children of the devil are: Anyone who does not do what is right is not a child of God; nor is anyone who does not love his brother.

I John 3:1-10

There came a man who was sent from God; his name was John. He came as a witness to testify concerning that light, so that through him all men might believe. He himself was not the light; he came only as a witness to the light. The true light that gives light to every man was coming into the world. He was in the world, and though the world was made through him, the world did not recognize him. He came to that which was his own, but his own did not receive him. Yet to all who received him, to those who believed in his name, he gave the right to become children of God.

John 1:6-12

"You should not be surprised at my saying, 'You must be born again.' The wind blows wherever it pleases. You hear its sound, but you cannot tell

25

where it comes from or where it is going. So it is with everyone born of the Spirit."

"How can this be?" Nicodemus asked.

"You are Israel's teacher," said Jesus, "and do you not understand these things? I tell you the truth, we speak of what we know, and we testify to what we have seen, but still you people do not accept our testimony. I have spoken to you of earthly things and you do not believe; how then will you believe if I speak of heavenly things? No one has ever gone into heaven except the one who came from heaven—the Son of Man. Just as Moses lifted up the snake in the desert, so the Son of Man must be lifted up, that everyone who believes in him may have eternal life.

"For God so loved the world that he gave his one and only Son, that whoever believes in him shall not perish but have eternal life."

John 3:7-16

"'For in him we live and move and have our being.' As some of your own poets have said, 'We are his offspring.'"

Acts 17:28

Be imitators of God, therefore, as dearly loved children. . .

Ephesians 5:1

He chose to give us birth through the word of truth,
that we might be a kind of firstfruits of all he created.

James 1:18

Be Childlike Yourself!

"Therefore, whoever humbles himself like this child
is the greatest in the kingdom of heaven."

Matthew 18:4

"Now, O LORD my God, you have made your servant
king in place of my father David. But I am only a little
child and do not know how to carry out my duties."

I Kings 3:7

He tends his flock like a shepherd:
He gathers the lambs in his arms
and carries them close to his heart;
he gently leads those that have young.

Isaiah 40:11

"Ah, Sovereign LORD," I said, "I do not know how to
speak; I am only a child."

But the LORD said to me, "Do not say, 'I am only
a child.' You must go to everyone I send you to and
say whatever I command you. Do not be afraid of
them, for I am with you and will rescue you,"
declares the LORD.

Jeremiah 1:6-8

In regard to evil be infants, but in your thinking be adults.

I Corinthians 14:20b

FOR PERSONAL PRAYER:

Praise to You, Lord, for granting me the privilege of parenting. Help me look to You daily, not only with praise for Your goodness, but with hunger for Your wisdom, as I seek to be the best parent I can be. Amen.

CHAPTER 2

'What does it mean to build a distinctly Christian home?'

That was the question Rebecca asked during a parenting seminar. "I suppose much of what we do will be very similar to what any of our neighbors are doing to raise their kids," she said. "But I have the feeling we'll stand out in significant ways too.

"We'll look to the Bible for our basic value system and our overall approach to family living. We know prayer will be an important part of our daily lives. We know too that when it comes to making key decisions, we'll be seeking God's leading. Because we're Christians, we're aware that every potential choice will affect, not only our own family, but the whole kingdom of God."

FOR MEMORY:

He will be the sure foundation for your times, a rich store of salvation and wisdom and knowledge; the fear of the LORD is the key to this treasure.

Isaiah 33:6

FOR SILENT REFLECTION:

- *What would I list as the four or five key principles upon which my home is built?*

- *In what ways do these principles express themselves in my family's words and actions?*

- *How does the way we make family decisions witness to our faith in God?*

- *How would I rate my personal level of commitment to doing God's will as a new parent?*

Build Your New Home on Biblical Principles

By wisdom a house is built,
and through understanding it is established. . .

Proverbs 24:3

He will be the sure foundation for your times,
a rich store of salvation and wisdom and knowledge;
the fear of the LORD is the key to this treasure.

Isaiah 33:6

"Therefore everyone who hears these words of mine and puts them into practice is like a wise man who built his house on the rock. The rain came down, the streams rose, and the winds blew and beat against that house; yet it did not fall, because it had its foundation on the rock. But everyone who hears these words of mine and does not put them into practice is like a foolish man who built his house on sand. The rain came down, the streams rose, and the winds blew and beat against that house, and it fell with a great crash."

When Jesus had finished saying these things, the crowds were amazed at his teaching. . .

Matthew 7:24-28

It has always been my ambition to preach the gospel where Christ was not known, so that I would not be building on someone else's foundation.

Romans 15:20

For no one can lay any foundation other than the one already laid, which is Jesus Christ. If any man builds on this foundation using gold, silver, costly stones, wood, hay or straw, his work will be shown for what it is, because the Day will bring it to light. It will be revealed with fire, and the fire will test the quality of each man's work. If what he has built survives, he will receive his reward.

I Corinthians 3:11-14

You also, like living stones, are being built into a spiritual house to be a holy priesthood, offering spiritual sacrifices acceptable to God through Jesus Christ.

I Peter 2:5

A Home Where Plans Are Based on Eternal Truths

And he told them this parable: "The ground of a certain rich man produced a good crop. He thought to himself, 'What shall I do? I have no place to store my crops.'

"Then he said, 'This is what I'll do. I will tear down my barns and build bigger ones, and there I will store all my grain and my goods. And I'll say to myself, "You have plenty of good things laid up for many years. Take life easy; eat, drink and be merry.'"

"But God said to him, 'You fool! This very night your life will be demanded from you. Then who will get what you have prepared for yourself?'

"This is how it will be with anyone who stores up things for himself but is not rich toward God."

Luke 12:16-21

The man who loves his life will lose it, while the man who hates his life in this world will keep it for eternal life.

John 12:25

Do not deceive yourselves. If any one of you thinks he is wise by the standards of this age, he should become a "fool" so that he may become wise. For the wisdom of this world is foolishness in God's sight. As it is written: "He catches the wise in their craftiness."

I Corinthians 3:18, 19

May I never boast except in the cross of our Lord Jesus Christ, through which the world has been crucified to me, and I to the world.

Galatians 6:14

"The kingdom of the world has become the kingdom

33

of our Lord and of his Christ, and he will reign for ever and ever."

Revelation 11:15b

Do not be afraid of those who kill the body but cannot kill the soul. Rather, be afraid of the One who can destroy both soul and body in hell.

Matthew 10:28

"There was a rich man who was dressed in purple and fine linen and lived in luxury every day. At his gate was laid a beggar named Lazarus, covered with sores and longing to eat what fell from the rich man's table. Even the dogs came and licked his sores.

"The time came when the beggar died and the angels carried him to Abraham's side. The rich man also died and was buried. In hell, where he was in torment, he looked up and saw Abraham far away, with Lazarus by his side. So he called to him, 'Father Abraham, have pity on me and send Lazarus to dip the tip of his finger in water and cool my tongue, because I am in agony in this fire.'

"But Abraham replied, 'Son, remember that in your lifetime you received your good things, while Lazarus received bad things, but now he is comforted here and you are in agony. And besides all this, between us and you a great chasm has been fixed, so that those who want to go from here to you cannot, nor can anyone cross over from there to us.'

"He answered, 'Then I beg you, father, send Lazarus to my father's house, for I have five brothers. Let him warn them, so that they will not also come to this place of torment.'

"Abraham replied, 'They have Moses and the Prophets; let them listen to them.'

"'No, father Abraham,' he said, 'but if someone from the dead goes to them, they will repent.'

"He said to him, 'If they do not listen to Moses and the Prophets, they will not be convinced even if someone rises from the dead.'"

Luke 16:19-31

A Home with the Bible at Its Center
All Scripture is God-breathed and is useful for teaching, rebuking, correcting and training in righteousness, so that the man of God may be thoroughly equipped for every good work.

II Timothy 3:16, 17

Do not let this Book of the Law depart from your mouth; meditate on it day and night, so that you may be careful to do everything written in it. Then you will be prosperous and successful.

Joshua 1:8

I have hidden your word in my heart
that I might not sin against you. . . .
I delight in your decrees;
I will not neglect your word.
Then I will answer the one who taunts me,
for I trust in your word. . . .
My comfort in my suffering is this:
Your promise preserves my life.

Psalm 119:11-16, 42-50

Finally, brothers, whatever is true, whatever is noble,
whatever is right, whatever is pure, whatever is love-
ly, whatever is admirable—if anything is excellent or
praiseworthy—think about such things.

Philippians 4:8

Your word is a lamp to my feet
and a light for my path. . . .
Sustain me according to your promise,
and I will live; do not let my hopes be dashed. . . .
Direct my footsteps according to your word;
let no sin rule over me. . . .
Your promises have been thoroughly tested,
and your servant loves them. . . .
I rise before dawn and cry for help;
I have put my hope in your word.
My eyes stay open through the watches of the night,
that I may meditate on your promises. . . .

Defend my cause and redeem me;
preserve my life according to your promise.

Psalm 119:105-154

For the word of God is living and active. Sharper
than any double-edged sword, it penetrates even to
dividing soul and spirit, joints and marrow; it judges
the thoughts and attitudes of the heart. Nothing in all
creation is hidden from God's sight Everything is
uncovered and laid bare before the eyes of him to
whom we must give account.

Hebrews 4:12, 13

A Home Built on God's Greatness
He stood, and shook the earth;
he looked, and made the nations tremble.
The ancient mountains crumbled
and the ageold hills collapsed.
His ways are eternal.
I saw the tents of Cushan in distress,
the dwellings of Midian in anguish.
Were you angry with the rivers, O LORD?
Was your wrath against the streams?
Did you rage against the sea
when you rode with your horses
and your victorious chariots?
You uncovered your bow,
you called for many arrows.

37

You split the earth with rivers;
the mountains saw you and writhed.
Torrents of water swept by;
the deep roared and lifted its waves on high.
Sun and moon stood still in the heavens
at the glint of your flying arrows,
at the lightning of your flashing spear.
In wrath you strode through the earth
and in anger you threshed the nations.
You came out to deliver your people,
to save your anointed one.

Habakkuk 3:6-13a

A Home Where the Love of God Flows
The LORD watches over all who love him,
but all the wicked he will destroy.

Psalm 145:20

I love those who love me,
and those who seek me find me.

Proverbs 8:17

"Whoever has my commands and obeys them, he is the one who loves me. He who loves me will be loved by my Father, and I too will love him and show myself to him."

John 14:21

So if you faithfully obey the commands I am giving you today—to love the LORD your God and to serve him with all your heart and with all your soul—then I will send rain on your land in its season, both autumn and spring rains, so that you may gather in your grain, new wine and oil. I will provide grass in the fields for your cattle, and you will eat and be satisfied.

Deuteronomy 11:13-15

"No eye has seen, no ear has heard, no mind has conceived what God has prepared for those who love him."

I Corinthians 2:9

Grace to all who love our Lord Jesus Christ with an undying love.

Ephesians 6:24

A Home Where Hospitality Reigns
Anyone who gives you a cup of water in my name because you belong to Christ will certainly not lose his reward.

Mark 9:41

I was hungry and you gave me something to eat, I was thirsty and you gave me something to drink, I was a stranger and you invited me in, I needed clothes and you clothed me, I was sick and you

39

looked after me, I was in prison and you came to visit me. . . . whatever you did for one of the least of these my brothers, you did for me.

Matthew 25:35-40

In everything I did, I showed you that by this kind of hard work we must help the weak, remembering the words the Lord Jesus himself said: "It is more blessed to give than to receive."

Acts 20:35

Share with God's people who are in need. Practice hospitality.

Romans 12:13

Suppose a brother or sister is without clothes and daily food. If one of you says to him, "Go, I wish you well; keep warm and well fed," but does nothing about his physical needs, what good is it?

James 2:15, 16

Offer hospitality to one another without grumbling. Each one should use whatever gift he has received to serve others, faithfully administering God's grace in its various forms.

I Peter 4:9, 10

If anyone has material possessions and sees his

40

brother in need but has no pity on him, how can the love of God be in him?

I John 3:17

Do not forget to entertain strangers, for by so doing some people have entertained angels without knowing it.

Hebrews 13:2

A Home of Kind Words and Helping Hands
Carry each other's burdens, and in this way you will fulfill the law of Christ. If anyone thinks he is something when he is nothing, he deceives himself. Each one should test his own actions. Then he can take pride in himself, without comparing himself to somebody else. . .

Galatians 6:2-4

Be completely humble and gentle; be patient, bearing with one another in love. Make every effort to keep the unity of the Spirit through the bond of peace.

Ephesians 4:2, 3

Speaking the truth in love, we will in all things grow up into him who is the Head, that is, Christ. From him the whole body, joined and held together by every supporting ligament, grows and builds itself up

41

in love, as each part does its work.

Ephesians 4:15, 16

Speak to one another with psalms, hymns and spiritual songs. Sing and make music in your heart to the Lord, always giving thanks to God the Father for everything, in the name of our Lord Jesus Christ.

Ephesians 5:19, 20

May the God who gives endurance and encouragement give you a spirit of unity among yourselves as you follow Christ Jesus, so that with one heart and mouth you may glorify the God and Father of our Lord Jesus Christ.

Romans 15:5, 6

A Home of Lasting Marital Commitment

Enjoy life with your wife, whom you love. . .

Ecclesiastes 9:9a

Submit to one another out of reverence for Christ. . . .

Husbands, love your wives, just as Christ loved the church and gave himself up for her to make her holy, cleansing her by the washing with water through the word, and to present her to himself as a radiant church, without stain or wrinkle or any other blemish, but holy and blameless. In this same way, husbands ought to love their wives as their own bodies. He who loves his wife loves himself. After all, no one ever hated his own body, but he feeds and cares for it, just as Christ does the church—for we are members of his body. "For this reason a man will leave his father and mother and be united to his wife, and the two will become one flesh." This is a profound mystery—but I am talking about Christ and the church. However, each one of you also must love his wife as he loves himself. . .

Ephesians 5:21-33a

It is God's will that you should be sanctified: that you should avoid sexual immorality.

I Thessalonians 4:3

Marriage should be honored by all, and the marriage bed kept pure, for God will judge the adulterer and all the sexually immoral.

Hebrews 13:4

Make every effort to live in peace with all men and to be holy; without holiness no one will see the Lord.

Hebrews 12:14

To the married I give this command (not I, but the Lord): A wife must not separate from her husband. But if she does, she must remain unmarried or else be

43

reconciled to her husband. And a husband must not divorce his wife.

To the rest I say this (I, not the Lord): If any brother has a wife who is not a believer and she is willing to live with him, he must not divorce her. And if a woman has a husband who is not a believer and he is willing to live with her, she must not divorce him. For the unbelieving husband has been sanctified through his wife, and the unbelieving wife has been sanctified through her believing husband. Otherwise your children would be unclean, but as it is, they are holy.

But if the unbeliever leaves, let him do so. A believing man or woman is not bound in such circumstances; God has called us to live in peace. How do you know, wife, whether you will save your husband? Or, how do you know, husband, whether you will save your wife?

I Corinthians 7:10-16

Be Ready: More Than One Child Brings Fighting!

"Meanwhile, the older son was in the field. When he came near the house, he heard music and dancing. So he called one of the servants and asked him what was going on. 'Your brother has come,' he replied, 'and your father has killed the fattened calf because he has him back safe and sound.'

"The older brother became angry and refused to

go in. So his father went out and pleaded with him. But he answered his father, 'Look! All these years I've been slaving for you and never disobeyed your orders. Yet you never gave me even a young goat so I could celebrate with my friends. But when this son of yours who has squandered your property with prostitutes comes home, you kill the fattened calf for him!'

"'My son,' the father said, 'you are always with me, and everything I have is yours. But we had to celebrate and be glad, because this brother of yours was dead and is alive again; he was lost and is found.'"

Luke 15:25-32

Cain and Abel

Adam lay with his wife Eve, and she became pregnant and gave birth to Cain. She said, "With the help of the LORD I have brought forth a man." Later she gave birth to his brother Abel. Now Abel kept flocks, and Cain worked the soil. In the course of time Cain brought some of the fruits of the soil as an offering to the LORD. But Abel brought fat portions from some of the firstborn of his flock. The LORD looked with favor on Abel and his offering, but on Cain and his offering he did not look with favor. So Cain was very angry, and his face was downcast.

Then the LORD said to Cain, "Why are you angry? Why is your face downcast? If you do what is right,

45

will you not be accepted? But if you do not do what is right, sin is crouching at your door; it desires to have you, but you must master it." Now Cain said to his brother Abel, "Let's go out to the field." And while they were in the field, Cain attacked his brother Abel and killed him. Then the LORD said to Cain, "Where is your brother Abel?" "I don't know," he replied. "Am I my brother's keeper?"

Genesis 4:1-8

Lot and Abram

Now Lot, who was moving about with Abram, also had flocks and herds and tents. But the land could not support them while they stayed together, for their possessions were so great that they were not able to stay together. And quarreling arose between Abram's herdsmen and the herdsmen of Lot. The Canaanites and Perizzites were also living in the land at that time.

So Abram said to Lot, "Let's not have any quarreling between you and me, or between your herdsmen and mine, for we are brothers. Is not the whole land before you? Let's part company. If you go to the left, I'll go to the right; if you go to the right, I'll go to the left." Lot looked up and saw that the whole plain of the Jordan was well watered, like the garden of the LORD, like the land of Egypt, toward Zoar. (This was before the LORD destroyed Sodom and Gomorrah.) So Lot chose for himself the whole plain of the Jordan and set out toward the east. The two men parted company: Abram lived in the land of Canaan, while Lot lived among the cities of the plain and pitched his tents near Sodom.

Genesis 13:5-12

Jephthah and His Brothers

Jephthah the Gileadite was a mighty warrior. His father was Gilead; his mother was a prostitute. Gilead's wife also bore him sons, and when they were grown up, they drove Jephthah away. "You are not going to get any inheritance in our family," they said, "because you are the son of another woman." So Jephthah fled from his brothers and settled in the land of Tob, where a group of adventurers gathered around him and followed him.

Judges 11:1-3

Judah and Israel

When the king crossed over to Gilgal, Kimham crossed with him. All the troops of Judah and half the troops of Israel had taken the king over. Soon all the men of Israel were coming to the king and saying to him, "Why did our brothers, the men of Judah, steal the king away and bring him and his household across the Jordan, together with all his men?" All the men of Judah answered the men of Israel, "We did this because the king is closely related to us. Why

47

are you angry about it? Have we eaten any of the king's provisions? Have we taken anything for ourselves?" Then the men of Israel answered the men of Judah, "We have ten shares in the king; and besides, we have a greater claim on David than you have. So why do you treat us with contempt? Were we not the first to speak of bringing back our king?" But the men of Judah responded even more harshly than the men of Israel.

II Samuel 19:40-43

... But Encourage Brothers and Sisters to Get Along

I appeal to you, brothers, in the name of our Lord Jesus Christ, that all of you agree with one another so that there may be no divisions among you and that you may be perfectly united in mind and thought.

I Corinthians 1:10

Aim for perfection, listen to my appeal, be of one mind, live in peace. And the God of love and peace will be with you.

II Corinthians 13:11b

Finally, all of you, live in harmony with one another; be sympathetic, love as brothers, be compassionate and humble.

I Peter 3:8

FOR PERSONAL PRAYER:

Lord, I want my parenting actions to bring honor to Your name. Help me to know when I'm pleasing You and when I'm falling short of Your will. May our family be a witness to Your goodness and grace. Amen.

CHAPTER 3

'What kinds of attitudes will I need for good parenting?'

I want to start right now to develop the attitudes that will make me a good parent over the years," said Margery. "I've seen too many examples of people losing their tempers with the kids or getting depressed about the hard work it takes to raise them.

"I want to be ready for the long haul ahead. I know it can be an enjoyable journey, but my parenting success—and joy—depends, to a great extent, upon the attitude I will choose on a daily basis."

> **FOR MEMORY:**
> Be completely humble and gentle; be patient, bearing with one another in love.
>
> *Ephesians 4:2*

FOR SILENT REFLECTION:

- *How patient were my parents with me when I was a child? What scenes stand out in my mind?*

- *How did my parents handle their anger around me when I was a child?*

- *Am I aware of any aspects of my personality that need special attention now that I am a parent?*

- *How would I rate myself on patience, perseverance, and the ability to control my moods?*

Develop Healthy Parenting Attitudes

Do not conform any longer to the pattern of this world, but be transformed by the renewing of your mind. Then you will be able to test and approve what God's will is—his good, pleasing and perfect will.

Romans 12:2

Learn to Control Your Anger

A patient man has great understanding,
but a quick-tempered man displays folly.

Proverbs 14:29

A quick-tempered man does foolish things,
and a crafty man is hated.

Proverbs 14:17

Better a patient man than a warrior,
a man who controls his temper than one who takes a city.

Proverbs 16:32

Grow in Patience

Be completely humble and gentle; be patient, bearing with one another in love. Make every effort to keep the unity of the Spirit through the bond of peace.

Ephesians 4:2, 3

53

Work on Teaching and Guiding Effectively

Fathers, do not exasperate your children; instead, bring them up in the training and instruction of the Lord.

Ephesians 6:4

Listen, my son, to your father's instruction
and do not forsake your mother's teaching.
They will be a garland to grace your head
and a chain to adorn your neck.

Proverbs 1:8, 9

My son, if you accept my words
and store up my commands within you,
turning your ear to wisdom
and applying your heart to understanding,
and if you call out for insight
and cry aloud for understanding,
and if you look for it as for silver
and search for it as for hidden treasure,
then you will understand the fear of the LORD
and find the knowledge of God.

Proverbs 2:1-5

Listen, my sons, to a father's instruction;
pay attention and gain understanding.
I give you sound learning,
so do not forsake my teaching.

When I was a boy in my father's house,
still tender, and an only child of my mother,
he taught me and said, "Lay hold of my words
with all your heart; keep my commands and you will
live.
Get wisdom, get understanding;
do not forget my words or swerve from them.
Do not forsake wisdom, and she will protect you;
love her,
and she will watch over you.
Wisdom is supreme; therefore get wisdom.
Though it cost all you have, get understanding.
Esteem her, and she will exalt you;
embrace her, and she will honor you.
She will set a garland of grace on your head
and present you with a crown of splendor."

Proverbs 4:1-9

Constantly Seek Parenting Wisdom from God

Let the wise listen and add to their learning,
and let the discerning get guidance. . . .

Proverbs 1:5

For the LORD gives wisdom,
and from his mouth come knowledge and understanding.

Proverbs 2:6

Blessed is the man who finds wisdom,
the man who gains understanding, fully.

Proverbs 3:13

The fear of the LORD is the beginning of wisdom,
and knowledge of the Holy One is understanding.

Proverbs 9:10

He who gets wisdom loves his own soul;
he who cherishes understanding prospers.

Proverbs 19:8

When Jesus spoke again to the people, he said, "I am
the light of the world. Whoever follows me will never
walk in darkness, but will have the light of life."

John 8:12

But God has revealed it to us by his Spirit. The Spirit
searches all things, even the deep things of God.

I Corinthians 2:10

The man without the Spirit does not accept the
things that come from the Spirit of God, for they are
foolishness to him, and he cannot understand them,
because they are spiritually discerned. The spiritual
man makes judgments about all things, but he himself is not subject to any man's judgment....

I Corinthians 2:14-15

56

We know also that the Son of God has come and has given us understanding, so that we may know him who is true. And we are in him who is true—even in his Son Jesus Christ. He is the true God and eternal life.

I John 5:20

Maintain a Spiritual Outlook

Since, then, you have been raised with Christ, set your hearts on things above, where Christ is seated at the right hand of God. Set your minds on things above, not on earthly things. For you died, and your life is now hidden with Christ in God. When Christ, who is your life, appears, then you also will appear with him in glory.

Put to death, therefore, whatever belongs to your earthly nature: sexual immorality, impurity, lust, evil desires and greed, which is idolatry. Because of these, the wrath of God is coming. You used to walk in these ways, in the life you once lived. But now you must rid yourselves of all such things as these: anger, rage, malice, slander, and filthy language from your lips. Do not lie to each other, since you have taken off your old self with its practices and have put on the new self, which is being renewed in knowledge in the image of its Creator. Here there is no Greek or Jew, circumcised or uncircumcised, barbarian, Scythian, slave or free, but Christ is all, and is in all.

Therefore, as God's chosen people, holy and dearly loved, clothe yourselves with compassion, kindness, humility, gentleness and patience. Bear with each other and forgive whatever grievances you may have against one another. Forgive as the Lord forgave you. And over all these virtues put on love, which binds them all together in perfect unity. Let the peace of Christ rule in your hearts, since as members of one body you were called to peace. And be thankful. Let the word of Christ dwell in you richly as you teach and admonish one another with all wisdom, and as you sing psalms, hymns and spiritual songs with gratitude in your hearts to God. And whatever you do, whether in word or deed, do it all in the name of the Lord Jesus, giving thanks to God the Father through him.

Wives, submit to your husbands, as is fitting in the Lord.

Husbands, love your wives and do not be harsh with them.

Children, obey your parents in everything, for this pleases the Lord.

Fathers, do not embitter your children, or they will become discouraged.

Colossians 3:1-21

Approach Parenting with a Servant Attitude
Your attitude should be the same as that of Christ Jesus: Who, being in very nature God, did not consider

equality with God something to be grasped,
but made himself nothing,
taking the very nature of a servant,
being made in human likeness.
And being found in appearance as a man,
he humbled himself and became obedient to death—
even death on a cross!
Therefore God exalted him to the highest place
and gave him the name that is above every name,
that at the name of Jesus every knee should bow,
in heaven and on earth and under the earth,
and every tongue confess that Jesus Christ is Lord,
to the glory of God the Father.
Therefore, my dear friends, as you have always
obeyed—not only in my presence, but now much
more in my absence—continue to work out your salvation with fear and trembling,
for it is God who works in you to will and to act
according to his good purpose.
Do everything without complaining or arguing, so
that you may become blameless and pure, children
of God without fault in a crooked and depraved generation, in which you shine like stars in the universe
as you hold out the word of life—in order that I may
boast on the day of Christ that I did not run or labor
for nothing.

Philippians 2:5-16

Lead Your Young Children to Personal Salvation

At that time the disciples came to Jesus and asked, "Who is the greatest in the kingdom of heaven?" He called a little child and had him stand among them. And he said: "I tell you the truth, unless you change and become like little children, you will never enter the kingdom of heaven. Therefore, whoever humbles himself like this child is the greatest in the kingdom of heaven. And whoever welcomes a little child like this in my name welcomes me. But if anyone causes one of these little ones who believe in me to sin, it would be better for him to have a large millstone hung around his neck and to be drowned in the depths of the sea. Woe to the world because of the things that cause people to sin! Such things must come, but woe to the man through whom they come! If your hand or your foot causes you to sin, cut it off and throw it away. It is better for you to enter life maimed or crippled than to have two hands or two feet and be thrown into eternal fire. And if your eye causes you to sin, gouge it out and throw it away. It is better for you to enter life with one eye than to have two eyes and be thrown into the fire of hell. See that you do not look down on one of these little ones. For I tell you that their angels in heaven always see the face of my Father in heaven."

Matthew 18:1-10

On the last and greatest day of the Feast, Jesus stood and said in a loud voice, "If anyone is thirsty, let him come to me and drink. Whoever believes in me, as the Scripture has said, streams of living water will flow from within him."

John 7:37, 38

You see, at just the right time, when we were still powerless, Christ died for the ungodly.

Very rarely will anyone die for a righteous man, though for a good man someone might possibly dare to die. But God demonstrates his own love for us in this: While we were still sinners, Christ died for us. Since we have now been justified by his blood, how much more shall we be saved from God's wrath through him! For if, when we were God's enemies, we were reconciled to him through the death of his Son, how much more, having been reconciled, shall we be saved through his life!

Romans 5:6-10

If you confess with your mouth, "Jesus is Lord," and believe in your heart that God raised him from the dead, you will be saved. For it is with your heart that you believe and are justified, and it is with your mouth that you confess and are saved.

Romans 10:9, 10

61

God Will Give You Strength for Your New Parenting Duties

He gives strength to the weary
and increases the power of the weak.

Isaiah 40:29

In the same way, the Spirit helps us in our weakness.
We do not know what we ought to pray for, but the
Spirit himself intercedes for us with groans that
words cannot express.

Romans 8:26

That is why, for Christ's sake, I delight in weakness-
es, in insults, in hardships, in persecutions, in diffi-
culties. For when I am weak, then I am strong.

II Corinthians 12:10

For to be sure, [Jesus] was crucified in weakness, yet
he lives by God's power. Likewise, we are weak in
him, yet by God's power we will live with him to
serve you.

II Corinthians 13:4

We are glad whenever we are weak but you are
strong; and our prayer is for your perfection.

II Corinthians 13:9

FOR PERSONAL PRAYER:

Lord, I have given You my soul, but I want You to take control of my mind too. When I feel anger bubbling up, give me Your peace; when I grow impatient, give me Your long-suffering. In every way, may I model Your loving care with my child. Amen.

CHAPTER 4

'What values should set the tone in my home?'

Hey, don't push your morality on me!' I hear that phrase so often these days," said Ted. "It seems to be society's ultimate argument for people's so-called right to do anything they please. But I don't plan to raise my kids in that kind of moral climate, no matter how popular it may be. I see the results of no ethical grounding in our society—and it scares me. I mean, look at the newspaper: Elementary school kids are now shooting each other for sports jackets!

"I'm not going to be one of those parents who can't point to any absolute values but then wonders why little junior seems to have no sense of right and wrong. I know my Lord calls for more responsible parenting than that."

FOR MEMORY:

Do not conform any longer to the pattern of this world, but be transformed by the renewing of your mind. Then you will be able to test and approve what God's will is—his good, pleasing and perfect will.

Romans 12:2

FOR SILENT REFLECTION:

- *What values stood out in my family of origin?*

- *What effect have my parents' values had on the way I've developed as an adult?*

- *What foundational values will inform the parenting decisions and actions in my own family?*

- *Could more fellowship with other Christian parents help me practice my values more consistently? How could I make more personal contact for this purpose?*

Model the Values You Believe In

Do not love the world or anything in the world. If anyone loves the world, the love of the Father is not in him. For everything in the world—the cravings of sinful man, the lust of his eyes and the boasting of what he has and does—comes not from the Father but from the world. The world and its desires pass away, but the man who does the will of God lives forever.

I John 2:15-17

For everyone born of God overcomes the world. This is the victory that has overcome the world, even our faith. Who is it that overcomes the world? Only he who believes that Jesus is the Son of God.

I John 5:4, 5

Therefore, prepare your minds for action; be self-controlled; set your hope fully on the grace to be given you when Jesus Christ is revealed.

I Peter 1:13

Noah: A Man Who Obeyed God's Instructions Perfectly

God saw how corrupt the earth had become, for all the people on earth had corrupted their ways. So God said to Noah, "I am going to put an end to all

67

people, for the earth is filled with violence because of them. I am surely going to destroy both them and the earth. So make yourself an ark of cypress wood; make rooms in it and coat it with pitch inside and out.

This is how you are to build it: The ark is to be 450 feet long, 75 feet wide and 45 feet high. Make a roof for it and finish the ark to within 18 inches of the top. Put a door in the side of the ark and make lower, middle and upper decks. I am going to bring floodwaters on the earth to destroy all life under the heavens, every creature that has the breath of life in it. Everything on earth will perish. But I will establish my covenant with you, and you will enter the ark—you and your sons and your wife and your sons' wives with you. You are to bring into the ark two of all living creatures, male and female, to keep them alive with you. Two of every kind of bird, of every kind of animal and of every kind of creature that moves along the ground will come to you to be kept alive. You are to take every kind of food that is to be eaten and store it away as food for you and for them."

Noah did everything just as God commanded him.

Genesis 6:12-22

Ananias: A Man Who Valued Money Too Highly
Now a man named Ananias, together with his wife Sapphira, also sold a piece of property. With his wife's full knowledge he kept back part of the

money for himself, but brought the rest and put it at the apostles' feet. Then Peter said, "Ananias, how is it that Satan has so filled your heart that you have lied to the Holy Spirit and have kept for yourself some of the money you received for the land? Didn't it belong to you before it was sold? And after it was sold, wasn't the money at your disposal? What made you think of doing such a thing? You have not lied to men but to God."

When Ananias heard this, he fell down and died. And great fear seized all who heard what had happened. Then the young men came forward, wrapped up his body, and carried him out and buried him.

Acts 5:1-6

Lois and Eunice: Women Who Encouraged Their Children for Christ

I have been reminded of your sincere faith, which first lived in your grandmother Lois and in your mother Eunice and, I am persuaded, now lives in you also.

II Timothy 1:5

Provide a Home Environment Based on God's Values

Conviction

King Nebuchadnezzar made an image of gold, ninety

69

feet high and nine feet wide, and set it up on the plain of Dura in the province of Babylon. . . .

Then the herald loudly proclaimed, "This is what you are commanded to do, O peoples, nations and men of every language: As soon as you hear the sound of the horn, flute, zither, lyre, harp, pipes and all kinds of music, you must fall down and worship the image of gold that King Nebuchadnezzar has set up. Whoever does not fall down and worship will immediately be thrown into a blazing furnace.". . .

"Is it true, Shadrach, Meshach and Abednego, that you do not serve my gods or worship the image of gold I have set up? Now when you hear the sound of the horn, flute, zither, lyre, harp, pipes and all kinds of music, if you are ready to fall down and worship the image I made, very good. But if you do not worship it, you will be thrown immediately into a blazing furnace. Then what god will be able to rescue you from my hand?" Shadrach, Meshach and Abednego replied to the king, "O Nebuchadnezzar, we do not need to defend ourselves before you in this matter. If we are thrown into the blazing furnace, the God we serve is able to save us from it, and he will rescue us from your hand, O king. But even if he does not, we want you to know, O king, that we will not serve your gods or worship the image of gold you have set up."

Daniel 3:1-18

One day as Jesus was standing by the Lake of Gennesaret, with the people crowding around him and listening to the word of God, he saw at the water's edge two boats, left there by the fishermen, who were washing their nets. He got into one of the boats, the one belonging to Simon, and asked him to put out a little from shore. Then he sat down and taught the people from the boat.

When he had finished speaking, he said to Simon, "Put out into deep water, and let down the nets for a catch."

Simon answered, "Master, we've worked hard all night and haven't caught anything. But because you say so, I will let down the nets."

When they had done so, they caught such a large number of fish that their nets began to break. So they signaled their partners in the other boat to come and help them, and they came and filled both boats so full that they began to sink.

When Simon Peter saw this, he fell at Jesus' knees and said, "Go away from me, Lord; I am a sinful man!" For he and all his companions were astonished at the catch of fish they had taken, and so were James and John, the sons of Zebedee, Simon's partners.

Then Jesus said to Simon, "Don't be afraid; from now on you will catch men." So they pulled their boats up on shore, left everything and followed him.

Luke 5:1-11

Perseverance

If a man is lazy,
the rafters sag;
if his hands are idle,
the house leaks.

Ecclesiastes 10:18

Do not be overcome by evil,
but overcome evil with good.

Romans 12:21

Jesus looked at them and said, "With man this is impossible, but with God all things are possible."

Matthew 19:26

He who stands firm to the end will be saved.

Matthew 24:13

Brothers . . . one thing I do: Forgetting what is behind and straining toward what is ahead, I press on toward the goal to win the prize for which God has called me heavenward in Christ Jesus.

Philippians 3:13, 14

You then, my son, be strong in the grace that is in Christ Jesus. And the things you have heard me say in the presence of many witnesses entrust to reliable men who will also be qualified to teach others. Endure hardship with us like a good soldier of Christ Jesus.

II Timothy 2:1-3

Then he said to them, "Suppose one of you has a friend, and he goes to him at midnight and says, 'Friend, lend me three loaves of bread, because a friend of mine on a journey has come to me, and I have nothing to set before him.' Then the one inside answers, 'Don't bother me. The door is already locked, and my children are with me in bed. I can't get up and give you anything.' I tell you, though he will not get up and give him the bread because he is his friend, yet because of the man's boldness he will get up and give him as much as he needs. . . .

"Ask and it will be given to you; seek and you will find; knock and the door will be opened to you. For everyone who asks receives; he who seeks finds; and to him who knocks, the door will be opened."

Luke 11:5-10

Then Jesus told them this parable: "Suppose one of you has a hundred sheep and loses one of them. Does he not leave the ninety-nine in the open country and go after the lost sheep until he finds it? And when he finds it, he joyfully puts it on his shoulders and goes home. Then he calls his friends and neighbors together and says, 'Rejoice with me; I have found my lost sheep.' I tell you that in the same way

73

there will be more rejoicing in heaven over one sinner who repents than over ninety-nine righteous persons who do not need to repent.

"Or suppose a woman has ten silver coins and loses one. Does she not light a lamp, sweep the house and search carefully until she finds it? And when she finds it, she calls her friends and neighbors together and says, 'Rejoice with me; I have found my lost coin.' In the same way, I tell you, there is rejoicing in the presence of the angels of God over one sinner who repents."

Luke 15:3-10

Cooperation

After I looked things over, I stood up and said to the nobles, the officials and the rest of the people, "Don't be afraid of them. Remember the Lord, who is great and awesome, and fight for your brothers, your sons and your daughters, your wives and your homes."

When our enemies heard that we were aware of their plot and that God had frustrated it, we all returned to the wall, each to his own work.

From that day on, half of my men did the work, while the other half were equipped with spears, shields, bows and armor.

Nehemiah 4:14-16a

Again, I tell you that if two of you on earth agree

74

about anything you ask for, it will be done for you by my Father in heaven. For where two or three come together in my name, there am I with them."

Matthew 18:19, 20

Carry each other's burdens, and in this way you will fulfill the law of Christ.

Galatians 6:2

I plead with Euodia and I plead with Syntyche to agree with each other in the Lord. Yes, and I ask you, loyal yokefellow, help these women who have contended at my side in the cause of the gospel, along with Clement and the rest of my fellow workers, whose names are in the book of life.

Philippians 4:2, 3

Unselfishness

So Abram went up from Egypt to the Negev, with his wife and everything he had, and Lot went with him. Abram had become very wealthy in livestock and in silver and gold. From the Negev he went from place to place until he came to Bethel, to the place between Bethel and Ai where his tent had been earlier and where he had first built an altar. There Abram called on the name of the LORD. Now Lot, who was moving about with Abram, also had flocks and herds and tents. But the land could not support them while they

75

stayed together, for their possessions were so great that they were not able to stay together. And quarreling arose between Abram's herdsmen and the herdsmen of Lot. The Canaanites and Perizzites were also living in the land at that time. So Abram said to Lot, "Let's not have any quarreling between you and me, or between your herdsmen and mine, for we are brothers. Is not the whole land before you? Let's part company. If you go to the left, I'll go to the right; if you go to the right, I'll go to the left."

Genesis 13:1-9

For I have come down from heaven not to do my will but to do the will of him who sent me.

John 6:38

And now, brothers, we want you to know about the grace that God has given the Macedonian churches. Out of the most severe trial, their overflowing joy and their extreme poverty welled up in rich generosity. For I testify that they gave as much as they were able, and even beyond their ability. Entirely on their own, they urgently pleaded with us for the privilege of sharing in this service to the saints.

II Corinthians 8:1-4

They overcame him by the blood of the Lamb and by the word of their testimony; they did not love their lives so much as to shrink from death.

Revelation12:11

Honesty

Do not steal.
Do not lie.
Do not deceive one another.

Leviticus 19:11

If you sell land to one of your countrymen or buy any from him, do not take advantage of each other. You are to buy from your countryman on the basis of the number of years since the Jubilee. And he is to sell to you on the basis of the number of years left for harvesting crops. When the years are many, you are to increase the price, and when the years are few, you are to decrease the price, because what he is really selling you is the number of crops. Do not take advantage of each other, but fear your God. I am the LORD your God.

Leviticus 25:14-17

You must have accurate and honest weights and measures, so that you may live long in the land the LORD your God is giving you. For the LORD your God detests anyone who does these things, anyone who deals dishonestly.

Deuteronomy 25:15, 16

Keep me from deceitful ways;
be gracious to me through your law.
I have chosen the way of truth;
I have set my heart on your laws.
I hold fast to your statutes, O LORD;
do not let me be put to shame.
I run in the path of your commands,
for you have set my heart free.
Teach me, O LORD, to follow your decrees;
then I will keep them to the end.
Give me understanding,
and I will keep your law and obey it with all my
heart.
Direct me in the path of your commands,
for there I find delight.
Turn my heart toward your statutes
and not toward selfish gain.
Turn my eyes away from worthless things;
preserve my life according to your word.

Psalm 119:29-37

Do not lie to each other, since you have taken off your
old self with its practices and have put on the new self,
which is being renewed in knowledge in the image of
its Creator.

Colossians 3:9, 10

Responsibility

The word of the LORD came to me:

"Son of man, speak to your countrymen and say to them: 'When I bring the sword against a land, and the people of the land choose one of their men and make him their watchman, and he sees the sword coming against the land and blows the trumpet to warn the people, then if anyone hears the trumpet but does not take warning and the sword comes and takes his life, his blood will be on his own head.

"'Since he heard the sound of the trumpet but did not take warning, his blood will be on his own head. If he had taken warning, he would have saved himself. But if the watchman sees the sword coming and does not blow the trumpet to warn the people and the sword comes and takes the life of one of them, that man will be taken away because of his sin, but I will hold the watchman accountable for his blood.'"

Ezekiel 33:1-6

"Again, it will be like a man going on a journey, who called his servants and entrusted his property to them. To one he gave five talents of money, to another two talents, and to another one talent, each according to his ability. Then he went on his journey. The man who had received the five talents went at once and put his money to work and gained five more. So also, the one with the two talents

79

gained two more. But the man who had received the one talent went off, dug a hole in the ground and hid his master's money.

"After a long time the master of those servants returned and settled accounts with them. The man who had received the five talents brought the other five. 'Master,' he said, 'you entrusted me with five talents. See, I have gained five more.'

"His master replied, 'Well done, good and faithful servant! You have been faithful with a few things; I will put you in charge of many things. Come and share your master's happiness!'

"The man with the two talents also came. 'Master,' he said, 'you entrusted me with two talents; see, I have gained two more.'

"His master replied, 'Well done, good and faithful servant! You have been faithful with a few things; I will put you in charge of many things. Come and share your master's happiness!'

"Then the man who had received the one talent came. 'Master,' he said, 'I knew that you are a hard man, harvesting where you have not sown and gathering where you have not scattered seed. So I was afraid and went out and hid your talent in the ground. See, here is what belongs to you.'

"His master replied, 'You wicked, lazy servant! So you knew that I harvest where I have not sown and gather where I have not scattered seed? Well then, you should have put my money on deposit with the bankers, so that when I returned I would have received it back with interest.

"'Take the talent from him and give it to the one who has the ten talents. For everyone who has will be given more, and he will have an abundance. Whoever does not have, even what he has will be taken from him. And throw that worthless servant outside, into the darkness, where there will be weeping and gnashing of teeth.'"

Matthew 25:14-30

Faith

Then Caleb silenced the people before Moses and said, "We should go up and take possession of the land, for we can certainly do it."

Numbers 13:30

Even though I walk
through the valley of the shadow of death,
I will fear no evil, for you are with me;
your rod and your staff, they comfort me.

Psalm 23: 4

"Be strong, do not fear; your God will come,
he will come with vengeance;
with divine retribution he will come to save you."

Isaiah 35: 4

81

"I tell you the truth, if you have faith as small as a mustard seed, you can say to this mountain, 'Move from here to there' and it will move. Nothing will be impossible for you."

Matthew 17:20b

"For nothing is impossible with God."

Luke 1:37

"So I say to you:
Ask and it will be given to you;
seek and you will find;
knock and the door will be opened to you."

Luke 11:9

Without faith it is impossible to please God, because anyone who comes to him must believe that he exists and that he rewards those who earnestly seek him.

Hebrews 11:6

For everyone born of God overcomes the world. This is the victory that has overcome the world, even our faith. This is the confidence we have in approaching God: that if we ask anything according to his will, he hears us. And if we know that he hears us—whatever we ask—we know that we have what we asked of him.

I John 5:4, 14, 15

FOR PERSONAL PRAYER:

Thank You, heavenly Father, for not leaving me to wonder about what pleases You. As I learn of Your values through Your Word, give me the courage to make them my own in daily living. Help my child see that Your will is the motivating factor in all I do. Amen.

CHAPTER 5

'How can I make discipline more than mere punishment?'

I know discipline isn't exactly supposed to be fun," said Sue. "But in my own childhood, with my parents, I don't remember it as being real instructive, either. In fact, I still tend to equate the word *discipline* mostly with a display of temper—accompanied by yelling or hitting.

"I know it'll be tough for me to break that pattern. I'm asking God to help me be an instructing and guiding parent rather than a punishing one."

FOR MEMORY:

Honor your father and your mother, as the LORD your God has commanded you, so that you may live long and that it may go well with you in the land the LORD your God is giving you.

Deuteronomy 5:16

FOR SILENT REFLECTION:

- *What methods of discipline did my parents use with me when I was a child?*

- *What kinds of discipline were most effective with me as a young child?*

- *What have I learned from my own childhood experiences of discipline and/or punishment?*

- *What is the best way for me to gain my child's growing respect?*

Growth Requires Discipline

"Blessed is the man whom God corrects;
so do not despise the discipline of the Almighty.
For he wounds, but he also binds up;
he injures, but his hands also heal.
From six calamities he will rescue you;
in seven no harm will befall you.
In famine he will ransom you from death,
and in battle from the stroke of the sword.
You will be protected from the lash of the tongue,
and need not fear when destruction comes.
You will laugh at destruction and famine,
and need not fear the beasts of the earth.
For you will have a covenant with the stones of the field,
and the wild animals will be at peace with you.
You will know that your tent is secure;
you will take stock of your property and find nothing missing.
You will know that your children will be many,
and your descendants like the grass of the earth.
You will come to the grave in full vigor,
like sheaves gathered in season."

Job 5:17-26

My son, do not make light of the Lord's discipline, and

do not lose heart when he rebukes you, because the Lord disciplines those he loves, and he punishes everyone he accepts as a son.

Endure hardship as discipline; God is treating you as sons. For what son is not disciplined by his father? If you are not disciplined (and everyone undergoes discipline), then you are illegitimate children and not true sons. . . . No discipline seems pleasant at the time, but painful. Later on, however, it produces a harvest of righteousness and peace for those who have been trained by it.

Hebrews 12:5b-11

Discipline Means Teaching Your Children . . .

Do not forget the things your eyes have seen or let them slip from your heart as long as you live. Teach them to your children and to their children after them. Remember the day you stood before the LORD your God at Horeb, when he said to me, "Assemble the people before me to hear my words so that they may learn to revere me as long as they live in the land and may teach them to their children."

Deuteronomy 4:9, 10

These commandments that I give you today are to be upon your hearts. Impress them on your children. Talk about them when you sit at home and when you walk along the road, when you lie down and when you get up. Tie them as symbols on your hands and bind them on your foreheads. Write them on the doorframes of your houses and on your gates.

Deuteronomy 6:6-9

Teach [God's commands] to your children, talking about them when you sit at home and when you walk along the road, when you lie down and when you get up.

Deuteronomy 11:19

I will open my mouth in parables,
I will utter hidden things, things from of old—
what we have heard and known,
what our fathers have told us.
We will not hide them from their children;
we will tell the next generation
the praiseworthy deeds of the LORD,
his power, and the wonders he has done.

Psalm 78:2-4

. . . But Sometimes You'll Need to Punish

Discipline your son,
and he will give you peace;
he will bring delight to your soul.

Proverbs 29:17

89

He who spares the rod hates his son,
but he who loves him is careful to discipline him.

Proverbs 13:24

Do not withhold discipline from a child;
if you punish him with the rod, he will not die.

Proverbs 23:13

Help Children Learn to Respect You

Each of you must respect his mother and father, and
you must observe my Sabbaths. I am the LORD your
God.

Leviticus 19:3

My son, keep your father's commands
and do not forsake your mother's teaching.

Proverbs 6:20

A wise son heeds his father's instruction,
but a mocker does not listen to rebuke.

Proverbs 13:1

A fool spurns his father's discipline,
but whoever heeds correction shows prudence.

Proverbs 15:5

Children, obey your parents in everything,

for this pleases the Lord.

Colossians 3:20

My son, if your heart is wise,
then my heart will be glad;
my inmost being will rejoice
when your lips speak what is right. . . .
Listen to your father, who gave you life,
and do not despise your mother when she is old. . . .
The father of a righteous man has great joy;
he who has a wise son delights in him.
May your father and mother be glad;
may she who gave you birth rejoice!
My son, give me your heart
and let your eyes keep to my ways. . . .

Proverbs 23:15-26

Help Children Learn Self-Control and Patience

He who loves pleasure will become poor;
whoever loves wine and oil will never be rich.

Proverbs 21:17

But mark this: There will be terrible times in the last
days. People will be lovers of themselves, lovers of
money, boastful, proud, abusive, disobedient to their
parents, ungrateful, unholy, without love, unforgiv-
ing, slanderous, without self-control, brutal, not

91

lovers of the good, treacherous, rash, conceited, lovers of pleasure rather than lovers of God. . . .

II Timothy 3:1-4

Therefore, prepare your minds for action; be self-controlled; set your hope fully on the grace to be given you when Jesus Christ is revealed. As obedient children, do not conform to the evil desires you had when you lived in ignorance. But just as he who called you is holy, so be holy in all you do; for it is written: "Be holy, because I am holy."

I Peter 1:13-16

That is why I am suffering as I am. Yet I am not ashamed, because I know whom I have believed, and am convinced that he is able to guard what I have entrusted to him for that day.

II Timothy 1:12

Help Children Say NO! to Temptation

Count yourselves dead to sin but alive to God in Christ Jesus. Therefore do not let sin reign in your mortal body so that you obey its evil desires.

Romans 6:11, 12

No temptation has seized you except what is common to man. And God is faithful; he will not let you be tempted beyond what you can bear. But when you are tempted, he will also provide a way out so that you can stand up under it.

I Corinthians 10:13

Finally, be strong in the Lord and in his mighty power. Put on the full armor of God so that you can take your stand against the devil's schemes. For our struggle is not against flesh and blood, but against the rulers, against the authorities, against the powers of this dark world and against the spiritual forces of evil in the heavenly realms. Therefore put on the full armor of God, so that when the day of evil comes, you may be able to stand your ground, and after you have done everything, to stand. Stand firm then, with the belt of truth buckled around your waist, with the breastplate of righteousness in place, and with your feet fitted with the readiness that comes from the gospel of peace. In addition to all this, take up the shield of faith, with which you can extinguish all the flaming arrows of the evil one. Take the helmet of salvation and the sword of the Spirit, which is the word of God. And pray in the Spirit on all occasions with all kinds of prayers and requests. With this in mind, be alert and always keep on praying for all the saints.

Ephesians 6:10-18

But the Lord is faithful, and he will strengthen and protect you from the evil one.

II Thessalonians 3:3

Be self-controlled and alert. Your enemy the devil prowls around like a roaring lion looking for someone to devour. Resist him, standing firm in the faith, because you know that your brothers throughout the world are undergoing the same kind of sufferings. And the God of all grace, who called you to his eternal glory in Christ, after you have suffered a little while, will himself restore you and make you strong, firm and steadfast.

I Peter 5:8-10

Help Children Make the Right Choices

This day I call heaven and earth as witnesses against you that I have set before you life and death, blessings and curses. Now choose life, so that you and your children may live. . . .

Deuteronomy 30:19

"But if serving the LORD seems undesirable to you, then choose for yourselves this day whom you will serve, whether the gods your forefathers served beyond the River, or the gods of the Amorites, in whose land you are living. But as for me and my household, we will serve the LORD."

Joshua 24:15

Then David said to God, "I have sinned greatly by doing this. Now, I beg you, take away the guilt of your servant. I have done a very foolish thing."

The LORD said to Gad, David's seer, "Go and tell David, 'This is what the LORD says: I am giving you three options. Choose one of them for me to carry out against you.'"

So Gad went to David and said to him, "This is what the LORD says: 'Take your choice: three years of famine, three months of being swept away before your enemies, with their swords overtaking you, or three days of the sword of the LORD—days of plague in the land, with the angel of the LORD ravaging every part of Israel.' Now then, decide how I should answer the one who sent me."

David said to Gad, "I am in deep distress. Let me fall into the hands of the LORD, for his mercy is very great; but do not let me fall into the hands of men."

I Chronicles 21:8-13

Help Children Develop Accountability

He who heeds discipline shows the way to life,
but whoever ignores correction leads others astray.

Proverbs 10:17

He who scorns instruction will pay for it,
but he who respects a command is rewarded.

Proverbs 13:13

The faithless will be fully repaid for their ways,
and the good man rewarded for his.

Proverbs 14:14

He who listens to a life-giving rebuke
will be at home among the wise.
He who ignores discipline despises himself,
but whoever heeds correction gains understanding.
The fear of the LORD teaches a man wisdom,
and humility comes before honor.

Proverbs 15:31-33

A man who remains stiff-necked after many rebukes
will suddenly be destroyed—without remedy.

Proverbs 29:1

A man's pride brings him low,
but a man of lowly spirit gains honor.

Proverbs 29:23

In Their Choice of Friends

Blessed is the man
who does not walk in the counsel of the wicked
or stand in the way of sinners

or sit in the seat of mockers.
But his delight is in the law of the LORD,
and on his law he meditates day and night.
He is like a tree planted by streams of water,
which yields its fruit in season
and whose leaf does not wither.
Whatever he does prospers.
Not so the wicked!
They are like chaff that the wind blows away.
Therefore the wicked will not stand in the judgment,
nor.sinners in the assembly of the righteous.
For the LORD watches over the way of the righteous,
but the way of the wicked will perish.

Psalm 1

A righteous man is cautious in friendship,
but the way of the wicked leads them astray.

Proverbs 12:26

A friend loves at all times,
and a brother is born for adversity.

Proverbs 17:17

A man of many companions may come to ruin,
but there is a friend who sticks closer than a brother.

Proverbs 18:24

He who loves a pure heart and whose speech is
gracious will have the king for his friend.

Proverbs 22:11

Do not make friends with a hot-tempered man,
do not associate with one easily angered.

Proverbs 22:24

Wounds from a friend can be trusted,
but an enemy multiplies kisses.

Proverbs 27:6

Do not forsake your friend and the friend of your
father,
and do not go to your brother's house when disaster
strikes you—
better a neighbor nearby than a brother far away.

Proverbs 27:10

In Their Chores, Large or Small

I went past the field of the sluggard,
past the vineyard of the man who lacks judgment;
thorns had come up everywhere,
the ground was covered with weeds,
and the stone wall was in ruins.
I applied my heart to what I observed
and learned a lesson from what I saw:
A little sleep, a little slumber,

a little folding of the hands to rest—
and poverty will come on you
like a bandit and scarcity like an armed man.

Proverbs 24:30-34

Do you not know that in a race all the runners run, but only one gets the prize? Run in such a way as to get the prize. Everyone who competes in the games goes into strict training. They do it to get a crown that will not last; but we do it to get a crown that will last forever. Therefore I do not run like a man running aimlessly; I do not fight like a man beating the air. No, I beat my body and make it my slave so that after I have preached to others, I myself will not be disqualified for the prize.

I Corinthians 9:24-27

Mind your own business and work with your hands, just as we told you, so that your daily life may win the respect of outsiders and so that you will not be dependent on anybody.

I Thessalonians 4:11, 12

For even when we were with you, we gave you this rule: "If a man will not work, he shall not eat."

We hear that some among you are idle. They are not busy; they are busybodies. Such people we command and urge in the Lord Jesus Christ to settle down and earn the bread they eat.

II Thessalonians 3:10-12

To Their Lord

"Not everyone who says to me, 'Lord, Lord,' will enter the kingdom of heaven, but only he who does the will of my Father who is in heaven."

Matthew 7:21

Do not merely listen to the word, and so deceive yourselves. Do what it says. Anyone who listens to the word but does not do what it says is like a man who looks at his face in a mirror and, after looking at himself, goes away and immediately forgets what he looks like. But the man who looks intently into the perfect law that gives freedom, and continues to do this, not forgetting what he has heard, but doing it—he will be blessed in what he does. If anyone considers himself religious and yet does not keep a tight rein on his tongue, he deceives himself and his religion is worthless. Religion that God our Father accepts as pure and faultless is this: to look after orphans and widows in their distress and to keep oneself from being polluted by the world.

James 1:22-27

FOR PERSONAL PRAYER:

Father, remind me that You discipline Your children because You love them, not because You delight in punishment. Help me to offer guidance and administer correction in the same spirit in which You lovingly lead me into my full potential. Amen.

CHAPTER 6

'How can I deal with the stress of added responsibilities?'

Matthew commented: "One of the greatest strains on us this past year has been the loss of income due to Sherry's staying home with the baby. We used to live pretty well on our two incomes. But now that's been cut in half and we're really feeling the financial pinch.

"The decision not to keep both of us working was tough for us. And it's not necessarily the right decision for everyone. We do see the parenting advantages; we're just having to find ways to overcome the disadvantages."

FOR MEMORY:

And God is able to make all grace abound to you, so that in all things at all times, having all that you need, you will abound in every good work.

II Corinthians 9:8

FOR SILENT REFLECTION:

• *To what extent was I aware of money strains in my family as I grew up?*

• *What other stresses did I sense in my parents?*

• *How do I hope to handle my internal tension around my own child?*

• *What part could my devotional life play in helping me deal with daily stress?*

Beware New-Parent Burnout!

Be merciful to me, LORD, for I am faint;
O LORD, heal me, for my bones are in agony.

Psalm 6:2

My knees give way from fasting;
my body is thin and gaunt.

Psalm 109:24

I lift up my eyes to the hills—
where does my help come from?
My help comes from the LORD,
the Maker of heaven and earth.
He will not let your foot slip—
he who watches over you will not slumber;
indeed, he who watches over Israel
will neither slumber nor sleep.
The LORD watches over you—
the LORD is your shade at your right hand;
the sun will not harm you by day,
nor the moon by night.
The LORD will keep you from all harm—
he will watch over your life;
the LORD will watch over your coming and going
both now and forevermore.

Psalm 121:1-8

The LORD is close to the brokenhearted
and saves those who are crushed in spirit.

Psalm 34:18

Cast your cares on the LORD and he will sustain you;
he will never let the righteous fall.

Psalm 55:22

Strengthen the feeble hands,
steady the knees that give way;
say to those with fearful hearts,
"Be strong, do not fear; your God will come.

Isaiah 35:3

When you pass through the waters,
I will be with you; and when you pass through the rivers,
they will not sweep over you.
When you walk through the fire,
you will not be burned;
the flames will not set you ablaze.

Isaiah 43:2

Struggling with Loss of Sleep from Crying Baby?

I lie down and sleep;
I wake again, because the LORD sustains me.

Psalm 3:5

I will lie down and sleep in peace,
for you alone, O LORD, make me dwell in safety.

Psalm 4:8

Stressed with Increased Pressure on the Family Budget?

The LORD hears the needy.

Psalm 69:33a

"The poor and needy search for water,
but there is none; their tongues are parched with thirst.
But I the LORD will answer them;
I, the God of Israel, will not forsake them."

Isaiah 41:17

Listen, my dear brothers: Has not God chosen those who are poor in the eyes of the world to be rich in faith and to inherit the kingdom he promised those who love him?

James 2:5

Trust in God's Provision

"Do not be afraid . . . I am your shield, your very great reward."

Genesis 15:1b

107

Your threshing will continue until grape harvest and the grape harvest will continue until planting, and you will eat all the food you want and live in safety in your land. I will grant peace in the land, and you will lie down and no one will make you afraid. I will remove savage beasts from the land, and the sword will not pass through your country. . . . You will still be eating last year's harvest when you will have to move it out to make room for the new.

Leviticus 26:5-10

"The eternal God is your refuge, and underneath are the everlasting arms. He will drive out your enemy before you, saying, 'Destroy him!' "

Deuteronomy 33:27

He will guard the feet of his saints,
but the wicked will be silenced in darkness.
It is not by strength that one prevails.

I Samuel 2:9

Fear the LORD, you his saints,
for those who fear him lack nothing.
The lions may grow weak and hungry,
but those who seek the LORD lack no good thing.

Psalm 34:9, 10

The LORD will keep you from all harm—

he will watch over your life;
the LORD will watch over your coming
and going both now and forevermore.

Psalm 121:7, 8

I was young and now I am old,
yet I have never seen the righteous forsaken
or their children begging bread.

Psalm 37:25

"I tell you the truth," Jesus replied, "no one who has left home or brothers or sisters or mother or father or children or fields for me and the gospel will fail to receive a hundred times as much in this present age (homes, brothers, sisters, mothers, children and fields—and with them, persecutions) and in the age to come, eternal life."

Mark 10:29, 30

Indeed, the very hairs of your head are all numbered. Don't be afraid; you are worth more than many sparrows.

Luke 12:7

And God is able to make all grace abound to you, so that in all things at all times, having all that you need, you will abound in every good work.

II Corinthians 9:8

And my God will meet all your needs according to his glorious riches in Christ Jesus.

Philippians 4:19

Cast all your anxiety on him because he cares for you.

I Peter 5:7

Use Your Money Wisely

Honor the LORD with your wealth,
with the firstfruits of all your crops;
then your barns will be filled to overflowing,
and your vats will brim over with new wine.

Proverbs 3:9-10

Do not wear yourself out to get rich;
have the wisdom to show restraint.
Cast but a glance at riches, and they are gone,
for they will surely sprout wings and fly off to the
sky like an eagle.

Proverbs 23:4, 5

Jesus sat down opposite the place where the offerings were put and watched the crowd putting their money into the temple treasury. Many rich people threw in large amounts. But a poor widow came and put in two very small copper coins, worth only a fraction of a penny.

Calling his disciples to him, Jesus said, "I tell you

the truth, this poor widow has put more into the treasury than all the others. They all gave out of their wealth; but she, out of her poverty, put in everything—all she had to live on."

Mark 12:41-44

Deal with Stress by Maintaining Your Physical Health

Through Retreating for Renewal

"Six days do your work, but on the seventh day do not work, so that your ox and your donkey may rest and the slave born in your household, and the alien as well, may be refreshed."

Exodus 23:12

Then [Jesus] got into the boat and his disciples followed him. Without warning, a furious storm came up on the lake, so that the waves swept over the boat. But Jesus was sleeping.

Matthew 8:23, 24

The apostles gathered around Jesus and reported to him all they had done and taught. Then, because so many people were coming and going that they did not even have a chance to eat, he said to them, "Come with me by yourselves to a quiet place and get some rest." So they went away by themselves in

111

a boat to a solitary place.

Mark 6:30-32

Through Handling Your Frustrations Calmly

In your anger do not sin;
when you are on your beds,
search your hearts and be silent.

Psalm 4:4

Do not let the sun go down while you are still angry.

Ephesians 4:26b

Surely it was for my benefit that I suffered such anguish. In your love you kept me from the pit of destruction; you have put all my sins behind your back.

Isaiah 38:17

Get rid of all bitterness, rage and anger, brawling and slander, along with every form of malice.

Ephesians 4:31

See to it that no one misses the grace of God and that no bitter root grows up to cause trouble and defile many.

Hebrews 12:15

Through Accepting Your Limitations

I have seen something else under the sun:

The race is not to the swift or the battle to the
strong,
nor does food come to the wise
or wealth to the brilliant or favor to the learned;
but time and chance happen to them all.
Moreover, no man knows when his hour will come:
As fish are caught in a cruel net,
or birds are taken in a snare,
so men are trapped by evil times
that fall unexpectedly upon them.

Ecclesiastes 9:11, 12

But we have this treasure in jars of clay to show that
this all-surpassing power is from God and not from
us. We are hard pressed on every side, but not
crushed; perplexed, but not in despair; persecuted,
but not abandoned; struck down, but not destroyed

II Corinthians 4:7-9

"Come to me, all you who are weary and burdened,
and I will give you rest. Take my yoke upon you and
learn from me, for I am gentle and humble in heart,
and you will find rest for your souls. For my yoke is
easy and my burden is light."

Matthew 11:28-30

Finally, be strong in the Lord and in his mighty
power.

Ephesians 6:10

Through Seeking God's Peace

You will keep in perfect peace him whose mind is steadfast, because he trusts in you.

Isaiah 26:3

He will be like a tree planted by the water
that sends out its roots by the stream.
It does not fear when heat comes;
its leaves are always green.
It has no worries in a year of drought
and never fails to bear fruit.

Jeremiah 17:8

"Peace I leave with you; my peace I give you. I do not give to you as the world gives. Do not let your hearts be troubled and do not be afraid."

John 14:27

"I have told you these things, so that in me you may have peace. In this world you will have trouble. But take heart! I have overcome the world."

John 16:33

For God is not a God of disorder but of peace. As in all the congregations of the saints. . . .

I Corinthians 14:33

For he himself is our peace, who has made the two

114

one and has destroyed the barrier, the dividing wall of hostility, by abolishing in his flesh the law with its commandments and regulations. His purpose was to create in himself one new man out of the two, thus making peace, and in this one body to reconcile both of them to God through the cross, by which he put to death their hostility. He came and preached peace to you who were far away and peace to those who were near.

Ephesians 2:14-17

Now may the Lord of peace himself give you peace at all times and in every way. The Lord be with all of you.
II Thessalonians 3:16

Through Asking God to Meet Your Needs
Ask of me, and I will make the nations your inheritance, the ends of the earth your possession.

Psalm 2:8

This is what the LORD says:
"Stand at the crossroads and look;
ask for the ancient paths,
ask where the good way is,
and walk in it,
and you will find rest for your souls.
But you said, "We will not walk in it."

Jeremiah 6:16

115

Ask the LORD for rain in the springtime;
it is the LORD who makes the storm clouds.
He gives showers of rain to men,
and plants of the field to everyone.

Zechariah 10:1

Until now you have not asked for anything in my name. Ask and you will receive, and your joy will be complete.

John 16:24

This is the confidence we have in approaching God: that if we ask anything according to his will, he hears us. And if we know that he hears us—whatever we ask—we know that we have what we asked of him.

I John 5:14, 15

Now to him who is able to do immeasurably more than all we ask or imagine, according to his power that is at work within us.

Ephesians 3:20

FOR PERSONAL PRAYER:

Lord, my new child brings me so much joy. But this great change in our lives has brought some new tensions too. Help me to see change as an adventure to be lived rather than a problem to be solved. Amen.

CHAPTER 7

'Where do I turn when I feel alone in my parenting task?'

I've begun to realize that it's not enough to read all the latest parenting books," said Julia. "Written advice is great but there is nothing like the warm touch of a friend who knows just exactly what you're going through.

"I told a friend the other day about a problem I was having with my baby. She knew exactly what was wrong. She'd gone through it before. We plan to get together often to pray and to compare notes about what it means to be a good mother."

FOR MEMORY:

God has said, "Never will I leave you; never will I forsake you."

Hebrews 13:5b

FOR SILENT REFLECTION:

- *Where do I turn when I feel lonely as a parent?*

- *How many people are available to me for parenting advice and guidance?*

- *How have I experienced the help of Christian fellowship in the past?*

- *Have I thoroughly discussed this issue with my spouse and parents?*

Feeling Lonely as a Parent?

I looked for sympathy, but there was none,
for comforters, but I found none.

Psalm 69:20b

I, the LORD, have called you in righteousness;
I will take hold of your hand.
I will keep you and will make you to be a covenant
for the people and a light for the Gentiles.

Isaiah 42:6

For the LORD will not reject his people;
he will never forsake his inheritance.

Psalm 94:14

Let In-Laws Help, If They Are Willing

Now Moses said to . . . [his] father-in-law, "We are set-
ting out for the place about which the LORD said, 'I
will give it to you.' Come with us and we will treat you
well, for the LORD has promised good things to Israel."

He answered, "No, I will not go; I am going back
to my own land and my own people."

But Moses said, "Please do not leave us. You
know where we should camp in the desert, and you
can be our eyes. If you come with us, we will share
with you whatever good things the LORD gives us."

Numbers 10:29-32

In the days when the judges ruled, there was a famine in the land, and a man from Bethlehem in Judah, together with his wife and two sons, went to live for a while in the country of Moab.

The man's name was Elimelech, his wife's name Naomi, and the names of his two sons were Mahlon and Kilion. They were Ephrathites from Bethlehem, Judah. And they went to Moab and lived there. Now Elimelech, Naomi's husband, died, and she was left with her two sons. They married Moabite women, one named Orpah and the other Ruth. After they had lived there about ten years, both Mahlon and Kilion also died, and Naomi was left without her two sons and her husband. . . .

Then Naomi said to her two daughters-in-law . . . "Return home, my daughters. Why would you come with me? Am I going to have any more sons, who could become your husbands? Return home, my daughters; I am too old to have another husband. Even if I thought there was still hope for me—even if I had a husband tonight and then gave birth to sons— would you wait until they grew up? Would you remain unmarried for them? No, my daughters. It is more bitter for me than for you, because the LORD'S hand has gone out against me!" At this they wept again. Then Orpah kissed her mother-in-law good-by, but Ruth clung to her.

"Look," said Naomi, "your sister-in-law is going

back to her people and her gods. Go back with her."

But Ruth replied, "Don't urge me to leave you or to turn back from you. Where you go I will go, and where you stay I will stay. Your people will be my people and your God my God. Where you die I will die, and there I will be buried. May the LORD deal with me, be it ever so severely, if anything but death separates you and me."

So Boaz took Ruth and she became his wife. Then he went to her, and the LORD enabled her to conceive, and she gave birth to a son. The women said to Naomi: "Praise be to the LORD, who this day has not left you without a kinsman-redeemer. May he become famous throughout Israel! He will renew your life and sustain you in your old age. For your daughter-in-law, who loves you and who is better to you than seven sons, has given him birth."

Then Naomi took the child, laid him in her lap and cared for him.

Ruth 1:1-17; 4:13-16

Build a Support Network of Other Parents
How good and pleasant it is
when brothers live together in unity! . . .
For there the LORD bestows his blessing,
even life forevermore.

Psalm 133:1-3

123

When Job's three friends, Eliphaz the Temanite, Bildad the Shuhite and Zophar the Naamathite, heard about all the troubles that had come upon him, they set out from their homes and met together by agreement to go and sympathize with him and comfort him. When they saw him from a distance, they could hardly recognize him; they began to weep aloud, and they tore their robes and sprinkled dust on their heads. Then they sat on the ground with him for seven days and seven nights. No one said a word to him, because they saw how great his suffering was.

Job 2:11-13

Be devoted to one another in brotherly love. Honor one another above yourselves.

Romans 12:10

Therefore encourage one another and build each other up, just as in fact you are doing. . . . And we urge you, brothers, warn those who are idle, encourage the timid, help the weak, be patient with everyone.

I Thessalonians 5:11-14

Find Support in Church Fellowship
Let us not give up meeting together, as some are in the habit of doing, but let us encourage one another— and all the more as you see the Day approaching.

Hebrews 10:25

The body is a unit, though it is made up of many parts; and though all its parts are many, they form one body. So it is with Christ. For we were all baptized by one Spirit into one body—whether Jews or Greeks, slave or free—and we were all given the one Spirit to drink.

Now the body is not made up of one part but of many. If the foot should say, "Because I am not a hand, I do not belong to the body," it would not for that reason cease to be part of the body. And if the ear should say, "Because I am not an eye, I do not belong to the body," it would not for that reason cease to be part of the body. If the whole body were an eye, where would the sense of hearing be? If the whole body were an ear, where would the sense of smell be?

But in fact God has arranged the parts in the body, every one of them, just as he wanted them to be. If they were all one part, where would the body be? As it is, there are many parts, but one body. The eye cannot say to the hand, "I don't need you!" And the head cannot say to the feet, "I don't need you!"

On the contrary, those parts of the body that seem to be weaker are indispensable, and the parts that we think are less honorable we treat with special honor. And the parts that are unpresentable are treated with special modesty, while our presentable parts need no special treatment. But God has combined the members of the body and has given greater honor to the parts that lacked it, so that there should be no division in the body, but that its parts should have equal concern for each other.

If one part suffers, every part suffers with it; if one part is honored, every part rejoices with it.

I Corinthians 12:12-26

They devoted themselves to the apostles' teaching and to the fellowship, to the breaking of bread and to prayer. Everyone was filled with awe, and many wonders and miraculous signs were done by the apostles. All the believers were together and had everything in common. Selling their possessions and goods, they gave to anyone as he had need. Every day they continued to meet together in the temple courts. They broke bread in their homes and ate together with glad and sincere hearts, praising God and enjoying the favor of all the people. And the Lord added to their number daily those who were being saved.

Acts 2:42-47

Support One Another with Your Gifts and Abilities

There are different kinds of gifts, but the same Spirit. There are different kinds of service, but the same Lord. There are different kinds of working, but the same God works all of them in all men.

Now to each one the manifestation of the Spirit is

given for the common good. To one there is given through the Spirit the message of wisdom, to another the message of knowledge by means of the same Spirit, to another faith by the same Spirit, to another gifts of healing by that one Spirit, to another miraculous powers, to another prophecy, to another distinguishing between spirits, to another speaking in different kinds of tongues, and to still another the interpretation of tongues. All these are the work of one and the same Spirit, and he gives them to each one, just as he determines.

I Corinthians 12:4-11

But to each one of us grace has been given as Christ apportioned it. . . .

It was he who gave some to be apostles, some to be prophets, some to be evangelists, and some to be pastors and teachers, to prepare God's people for works of service, so that the body of Christ may be built up until we all reach unity in the faith and in the knowledge of the Son of God and become mature, attaining to the whole measure of the fullness of Christ.

Then we will no longer be infants, tossed back and forth by the waves, and blown here and there by every wind of teaching and by the cunning and craftiness of men in their deceitful scheming. Instead, speaking the truth in love, we will in all things grow

127

up into him who is the Head, that is, Christ. From him the whole body, joined and held together by every supporting ligament, grows and builds itself up in love, as each part does its work.

Ephesians 4:7-16

Above all, love each other deeply, because love covers over a multitude of sins. Offer hospitality to one another without grumbling. Each one should use whatever gift he has received to serve others, faithfully administering God's grace in its various forms. If anyone speaks, he should do it as one speaking the very words of God. If anyone serves, he should do it with the strength God provides, so that in all things God may be praised through Jesus Christ. To him be the glory and the power for ever and ever. Amen.

I Peter 4:8-11

Learn to Fellowship with God in Prayer

The LORD is near to all who call on him,
to all who call on him in truth.
He fulfills the desires of those who fear him;
he hears their cry and saves them.

Psalm 145:18, 19

Then you will call, and the LORD will answer;
you will cry for help, and he will say: Here am I.

If you do away with the yoke of oppression,
with the pointing finger and malicious talk.

Isaiah 58:9

Let us draw near to God with a sincere heart in full assurance of faith, having our hearts sprinkled to cleanse us from a guilty conscience and having our bodies washed with pure water.

Hebrews 10:22

"Ask and it will be given to you; seek and you will find; knock and the door will be opened to you. For everyone who asks receives; he who seeks finds; and to him who knocks, the door will be opened.

Which of you, if his son asks for bread, will give him a stone? Or if he asks for a fish, will give him a snake? If you, then, though you are evil, know how to give good gifts to your children, how much more will your Father in heaven give good gifts to those who ask him!"

Matthew 7:7-11

Your Heavenly Father Hears Your Prayers
This is the confidence we have in approaching God: that if we ask anything according to his will, he hears us.

I John 5:14

129

Before they call I will answer;
while they are still speaking I will hear.

Isaiah 65:24

"Call to me and I will answer you and tell you great
and unsearchable things you do not know."

Jeremiah 33:3

If any of you lacks wisdom, he should ask God, who
gives generously to all without finding fault, and it
will be given to him.

James 1:5

Then Hannah prayed and said: "My heart rejoices in
the LORD; in the LORD my horn is lifted high. My
mouth boasts over my enemies, for I delight in your
deliverance." And the LORD was gracious to Hannah;
she conceived and gave birth to three sons and two
daughters. Meanwhile, the boy Samuel grew up in
the presence of the LORD.

I Samuel 2:1, 21

If my people, who are called by my name, will humble themselves and pray and seek my face and turn
from their wicked ways, then will I hear from heaven
and will forgive their sin and will heal their land.

II Chronicles 7:14

Yet if you devote your heart to him
and stretch out your hands to him,
if you put away the sin that is in your hand
and allow no evil to dwell in your tent,
then you will lift up your face without shame;
you will stand firm and without fear.
You will surely forget your trouble,
recalling it only as waters gone by.
Life will be brighter than noonday,
and darkness will become like morning.
You will be secure, because there is hope;
you will look about you and take your rest in safety.
You will lie down, with no one to make you afraid,
and many will court your favor.

Job 11:13-19

Who among you fears the LORD
and obeys the word of his servant?
Let him who walks in the dark,
who has no light, trust in the name of the LORD
and rely on his God.

Isaiah 50:10

Your Savior Prays for You

Jesus . . . looked toward heaven and prayed . . . "I
pray for them. I am not praying for the world, but for
those you have given me, for they are yours. All I have
is yours, and all you have is mine. And glory has come

131

to me through them. I will remain in the world no longer, but they are still in the world, and I am coming to you. Holy Father, protect them by the power of your name—the name you gave me—so that they may be one as we are one. While I was with them, I protected them and kept them safe by that name you gave me. None has been lost except the one doomed to destruction so that Scripture would be fulfilled.

"I am coming to you now, but I say these things while I am still in the world, so that they may have the full measure of my joy within them. I have given them your word and the world has hated them, for they are not of the world any more than I am of the world. My prayer is not that you take them out of the world but that you protect them from the evil one."

John 17:1, 9-15

Therefore he is able to save completely those who come to God through him, because he always lives to intercede for them. Such a high priest meets our need—one who is holy, blameless, pure, set apart from sinners, exalted above the heavens. Unlike the other high priests, he does not need to offer sacrifices day after day, first for his own sins, and then for the sins of the people. He sacrificed for their sins once for all when he offered himself.

Hebrews 7:25-27

For Christ did not enter a man-made sanctuary that was only a copy of the true one; he entered heaven itself, now to appear for us in God's presence. Nor did he enter heaven to offer himself again and again, the way the high priest enters the Most Holy Place every year with blood that is not his own. Then Christ would have had to suffer many times since the creation of the world. But now he has appeared once for all at the end of the ages to do away with sin by the sacrifice of himself. Just as man is destined to die once, and after that to face judgment, so Christ was sacrificed once to take away the sins of many people; and he will appear a second time, not to bear sin, but to bring salvation to those who are waiting for him.

Hebrews 9:24-28

My dear children, I write this to you so that you will not sin. But if anybody does sin, we have one who speaks to the Father in our defense—Jesus Christ, the Righteous One.

1 John 2:1

The Holy Spirit Stays with You
"And I will do whatever you ask in my name, so that the Son may bring glory to the Father. You may ask me for anything in my name, and I will do it. If you love me, you will obey what I command. And I will ask the Father, and he will give you another Counselor

133

to be with you forever—the Spirit of truth. The world cannot accept him, because it neither sees him nor knows him. But you know him, for he lives with you and will be in you."

John 14:13-17

"All this I have spoken while still with you. But the Counselor, the Holy Spirit, whom the Father will send in my name, will teach you all things and will remind you of everything I have said to you. Peace I leave with you; my peace I give you. I do not give to you as the world gives. Do not let your hearts be troubled and do not be afraid."

John 14:25-27

"Now I am going to him who sent me, yet none of you asks me, 'Where are you going?' Because I have said these things, you are filled with grief. But I tell you the truth: It is for your good that I am going away. Unless I go away, the Counselor will not come to you; but if I go, I will send him to you. When he comes, he will convict the world of guilt in regard to sin and righteousness and judgment: in regard to sin, because men do not believe in me; in regard to righteousness, because I am going to the Father, where you can see me no longer; and in regard to judgment, because the prince of this world now stands condemned.

"I have much more to say to you, more than you can

now bear. But when he, the Spirit of truth, comes, he will guide you into all truth. He will not speak on his own; he will speak only what he hears, and he will tell you what is yet to come. He will bring glory to me by taking from what is mine and making it known to you. All that belongs to the Father is mine. That is why I said the Spirit will take from what is mine and make it known to you."

John 16:5-15

And afterward, I will pour out my Spirit on all people.
Your sons and daughters will prophesy,
your old men will dream dreams,
your young men will see visions.
Even on my servants, both men and women,
I will pour out my Spirit in those days.
I will show wonders in the heavens and on the earth,
blood and fire and billows of smoke.
The sun will be turned to darkness
and the moon to blood
before the coming of the great and dreadful day of the LORD.
And everyone who calls on the name of the LORD will be saved;
for on Mount Zion and in Jerusalem there will be deliverance,
as the LORD has said, among the survivors whom the LORD calls.

Joel 2:28-32

135

"If you then, though you are evil, know how to give good gifts to your children, how much more will your Father in heaven give the Holy Spirit to those who ask him!"

Luke 11:13

On the last and greatest day of the Feast, Jesus stood and said in a loud voice, "If anyone is thirsty, let him come to me and drink. Whoever believes in me, as the Scripture has said, streams of living water will flow from within him." By this he meant the Spirit, whom those who believed in him were later to receive. Up to that time the Spirit had not been given, since Jesus had not yet been glorified.

John 7:37-39

FOR PERSONAL PRAYER:

Father, although I love my child, sometimes I get lonely for other adults. I need to know that You are close, and I need to have others close too. Turn my loneliness into the energy I need to reach out for new friends. Amen.

=== CHAPTER 8 ===

'Will God really provide all I need for this task?'

S ometimes I do question God's provision," said Rachel. "I focus on the things I seem to need so badly and I don't immediately see how God is at work as a provider. Yet at those times I can stop and ask myself: What do I really need? What is for my best in this situation?

"I'm sure that sometimes I need patience more than I need money. And often I need perseverance more than I need rest. So God provides, according to His wisdom and my best interests. I'd just like to be more aware, daily, of how God really is taking care of me."

FOR MEMORY:

Do not be anxious about anything, but in everything, by prayer and petition, with thanksgiving, present your requests to God.

Philippians 4:6

FOR SILENT REFLECTION:

- *Did my own parents look to God as their ultimate provider in life?*

- *How well am I able to handle apparent instability or risk in life?*

- *How have I found God to be a faithful provider in my past?*

- *In what specific kinds of situations do I need my faith in God's provision strengthened?*

God Is the Ultimate Provider

"I tell you, do not worry about your life, what you will eat or drink; or about your body, what you will wear. Is not life more important than food, and the body more important than clothes? Look at the birds of the air; they do not sow or reap or store away in barns, and yet your heavenly Father feeds them. Are you not much more valuable than they? Who of you by worrying can add a single hour to his life?

"And why do you worry about clothes? See how the lilies of the field grow. They do not labor or spin. Yet I tell you that not even Solomon in all his splendor was dressed like one of these. If that is how God clothes the grass of the field, which is here today and tomorrow is thrown into the fire, will he not much more clothe you, O you of little faith? So do not worry, saying, 'What shall we eat?' or 'What shall we drink?' or 'What shall we wear?' For the pagans run after all these things, and your heavenly Father knows that you need them. But seek first his kingdom and his righteousness, and all these things will be given to you as well. Therefore do not worry about tomorrow, for tomorrow will worry about itself. Each day has enough trouble of its own."

Matthew 6:25-34

Do not be anxious about anything, but in everything, by prayer and petition, with thanksgiving, present your requests to God. And the peace of God, which transcends all understanding, will guard your hearts and your minds in Christ Jesus. . . . I am not saying this because I am in need, for I have learned to be content whatever the circumstances. I know what it is to be in need, and I know what it is to have plenty. I have learned the secret of being content in any and every situation, whether well fed or hungry, whether living in plenty or in want.

Philippians 4:6-12

The Names of God the Father Inspire Confidence

The Lord Is Our Righteousness
In his days Judah will be saved and Israel will live in safety.

This is the name by which he will be called: The LORD Our Righteousness.

Jeremiah 23:6

The Lord Makes Us Holy
Say to the Israelites, "You must observe my Sabbaths. This will be a sign between me and you for the generations to come, so you may know that I am the LORD, who makes you holy."

Exodus 31:13

The Lord Heals

He said, "If you listen carefully to the voice of the LORD your God and do what is right in his eyes, if you pay attention to his commands and keep all his decrees, I will not bring on you any of the diseases I brought on the Egyptians, for I am the LORD, who heals you."

Exodus 15:26

The Lord Is Our Banner

So Joshua overcame the Amalekite army with the sword. Then the LORD said to Moses, "Write this on a scroll as something to be remembered and make sure that Joshua hears it, because I will completely blot out the memory of Amalek from under heaven." Moses built an altar and called it The LORD is my Banner.

Exodus 17:13-15

The Lord Gives Peace

So Gideon built an altar to the LORD there and called it The LORD is Peace.

Judges 6:24

The Lord Is Present

The distance all around will be 18,000 cubits. And the name of the city from that time on will be: the LORD is there.

Ezekiel 48:35

141

The Lord Is the Redeemer

This is what the LORD says—your Redeemer, who formed you in the womb: I am the LORD, who has made all things, who alone stretched out the heavens, who spread out the earth by myself.

Isaiah 44:24

The Lord Is Infinite

God said to Moses, "I AM Who I AM. This is what you are to say to the Israelites: 'I AM has sent me to you.'"

Exodus 3:14

The Titles of God the Son Offer Encouragement

I Am the Bread of Life

Then Jesus declared, "I am the bread of life. He who comes to me will never go hungry. . . . But as I told you, you have seen me and still you do not believe. All that the Father gives me will come to me, and whoever comes to me I will never drive away. For I have come down from heaven not to do my will but to do the will of him who sent me. And this is the will of him who sent me, that I shall lose none of all that he has given me, but raise them up at the last day. For my Father's will is that everyone who looks to the Son and believes in him shall have eternal life, and I will raise him up at the last day."

John 6:35-40

I Am the Light of the World

When Jesus spoke again to the people, he said, "I am the light of the world. Whoever follows me will never walk in darkness, but will have the light of life."

John 8:12

"As long as it is day, we must do the work of him who sent me. Night is coming, when no one can work. While I am in the world, I am the light of the world."

John 9:4, 5

I Am the Gate of Salvation

Therefore Jesus said again, "I tell you the truth, I am the gate for the sheep. All who ever came before me were thieves and robbers, but the sheep did not listen to them. I am the gate; whoever enters through me will be saved. He will come in and go out, and find pasture. The thief comes only to steal and kill and destroy; I have come that they may have life, and have it to the full."

John 10:7-10

I Am the Good Shepherd

"I am the good shepherd. The good shepherd lays down his life for the sheep. The hired hand is not the shepherd who owns the sheep. So when he sees the wolf coming, he abandons the sheep and runs away. Then the wolf attacks the flock and scatters it. The man runs away because he is a hired hand and cares nothing for the sheep.

"I am the good shepherd; I know my sheep and my sheep know me—just as the Father knows me and I know the Father—and I lay down my life for the sheep. I have other sheep that are not of this sheep pen. I must bring them also. They too will listen to my voice, and there shall be one flock and one shepherd. The reason my Father loves me is that I lay down my life—only to take it up again. No one takes it from me, but I lay it down of my own accord. I have authority to lay it down and authority to take it up again. This command I received from my Father."

John 10:11-18

I Am the Resurrection and the Life

"Lord," Martha said to Jesus, "if you had been here, my brother would not have died. But I know that even now God will give you whatever you ask." Jesus said to her, "Your brother will rise again." Martha answered, "I know he will rise again in the resurrection at the last day." Jesus said to her, "I am the resurrection and the life. He who believes in me will live, even though he dies; and whoever lives and believes in me will never die. Do you believe this?"

John 11:21-26

I Am the True Vine

"I am the true vine, and my Father is the gardener. He cuts off every branch in me that bears no fruit, while every branch that does bear fruit he prunes so that it will be even more fruitful. You are already clean because of the word I have spoken to you. Remain in me, and I will remain in you. No branch can bear fruit by itself; it must remain in the vine. Neither can you bear fruit unless you remain in me. I am the vine; you are the branches. If a man remains in me and I in him, he will bear much fruit; apart from me you can do nothing. If anyone does not remain in me, he is like a branch that is thrown away and withers; such branches are picked up, thrown into the fire and burned. If you remain in me and my words remain in you, ask whatever you wish, and it will be given you."

John 15:1-7

He Is the Parent of All Parents

He Is Good and Loving

How great is your goodness,
which you have stored up for those who fear you,
which you bestow in the sight of men
on those who take refuge in you.
In the shelter of your presence you hide them
from the intrigues of men;

145

in your dwelling you keep them safe
from accusing tongues.

Psalm 31:19, 20

But he lifted the needy out of their affliction
and increased their families like flocks.
The upright see and rejoice,
but all the wicked shut their mouths.
Whoever is wise, let him heed these things
and consider the great love of the LORD.

Psalm 107:41-43

For I am convinced that neither death nor life, neither
angels nor demons, neither the present nor the future,
nor any powers, neither height nor depth, nor anything else in all creation, will be able to separate us
from the love of God that is in Christ Jesus our Lord.

Romans 8:38, 39

How great is the love the Father has lavished on us,
that we should be called children of God! And that is
what we are!

I John 3:1a

He Is Accepting
[He] accepts men from every nation who fear him
and do what is right.

Acts 10:35

146

Praise be to the God and Father of our Lord Jesus Christ, who has blessed us in the heavenly realms with every spiritual blessing in Christ. For he chose us in him before the creation of the world to be holy and blameless in his sight. In love he predestined us to be adopted as his sons through Jesus Christ, in accordance with his pleasure and will—to the praise of his glorious grace, which he has freely given us in the One he loves.

Ephesians 1:3-6

But because of his great love for us, God, who is rich in mercy, made us alive with Christ even when we were dead in transgressions—it is by grace you have been saved. And God raised us up with Christ and seated us with him in the heavenly realms in Christ Jesus, in order that in the coming ages he might show the incomparable riches of his grace, expressed in his kindness to us in Christ Jesus. For it is by grace you have been saved, through faith—and this not from yourselves, it is the gift of God—not by works, so that no one can boast.

Ephesians 2:4-9

You also, like living stones, are being built into a spiritual house to be a holy priesthood, offering spiritual sacrifices acceptable to God through Jesus Christ.

I Peter 2:5

He Adopts

If those who live by law are heirs, faith has no value and the promise is worthless, because law brings wrath. And where there is no law there is no transgression.

Therefore, the promise comes by faith, so that it may be by grace and may be guaranteed to all Abraham's offspring—not only to those who are of the law but also to those who are of the faith of Abraham. He is the father of us all. As it is written: "I have made you a father of many nations." He is our father in the sight of God, in whom he believed—the God who gives life to the dead and calls things that are not as though they were.

Against all hope, Abraham in hope believed and so became the father of many nations, just as it had been said to him, "So shall your offspring be."

Without weakening in his faith, he faced the fact that his body was as good as dead—since he was about a hundred years old—and that Sarah's womb was also dead. Yet he did not waver through unbelief regarding the promise of God, but was strengthened in his faith and gave glory to God, being fully persuaded that God had power to do what he had promised. This is why "it was credited to him as righteousness."

Romans 4:14-22

So also, when we were children, we were in slavery

under the basic principles of the world. But when the time had fully come, God sent his Son, born of a woman, born under law, to redeem those under law, that we might receive the full rights of sons. Because you are sons, God sent the Spirit of his Son into our hearts, the Spirit who calls out, "Abba, Father." So you are no longer a slave, but a son; and since you are a son, God has made you also an heir.

Galatians 4:3-7

He Comforts

For he wounds,
but he also binds up;
he injures,
but his hands also heal.

Job 5:18

Praise the LORD.
How good it is to sing praises to our God,
how pleasant and fitting to praise him!
The LORD builds up Jerusalem;
he gathers the exiles of Israel.
He heals the brokenhearted
and binds up their wounds.

Psalm 147:1-3

He tends his flock like a shepherd:
He gathers the lambs in his arms
and carries them close to his heart;

149

he gently leads those that have young.

Isaiah 40:11

I, even I, am he who comforts you.
Who are you that you fear mortal men,
the sons of men,
who are but grass.

Isaiah 51:12

As a mother comforts her child,
so will I comfort you.

Isaiah 66:13a

"But all who devour you will be devoured;
all your enemies will go into exile.
Those who plunder you will be plundered;
all who make spoil of you I will despoil.
But I will restore you to health and heal your wounds,"
declares the LORD, "because you are called an outcast,
Zion for whom no one cares."

Jeremiah 30:16, 17

Praise be to the God and Father of our Lord Jesus
Christ, the Father of compassion and the God of all
comfort, who comforts us in all our troubles, so that
we can comfort those in any trouble with the comfort we ourselves have received from God.

I Corinthians 1:3, 4

At one time we too were foolish, disobedient, deceived and enslaved by all kinds of passions and pleasures. We lived in malice and envy, being hated and hating one another. But when the kindness and love of God our Savior appeared, he saved us, not because of righteous things we had done, but because of his mercy. He saved us through the washing of rebirth and renewal by the Holy Spirit, whom he poured out on us generously through Jesus Christ our Savior, so that, having been justified by his grace, we might become heirs having the hope of eternal life.

Titus 3:3-7

He Protects and Encourages

"What do you think? If a man owns a hundred sheep, and one of them wanders away, will he not leave the ninety-nine on the hills and go to look for the one that wandered off? And if he finds it, I tell you the truth, he is happier about that one sheep than about the ninety-nine that did not wander off. In the same way your Father in heaven is not willing that any of these little ones should be lost."

Matthew 18:12-14

May our Lord Jesus Christ himself and God our Father, who loved us and by his grace gave us eternal encouragement and good hope, encourage your hearts and strengthen you in every good deed and word.

II Thessalonians 2:16, 17

He Provides Us with Good Things in Life

Then he said to them, "Suppose one of you has a friend, and he goes to him at midnight and says, 'Friend, lend me three loaves of bread, because a friend of mine on a journey has come to me, and I have nothing to set before him.'

"Then the one inside answers, 'Don't bother me. The door is already locked, and my children are with me in bed. I can't get up and give you anything.'

"I tell you, though he will not get up and give him the bread because he is his friend, yet because of the man's boldness he will get up and give him as much as he needs. So I say to you: Ask and it will be given to you; seek and you will find; knock and the door will be opened to you. For everyone who asks receives; he who seeks finds; and to him who knocks, the door will be opened.

"Which of you fathers, if your son asks for a fish, will give him a snake instead? Or if he asks for an egg, will give him a scorpion? If you then, though you are evil, know how to give good gifts to your children, how much more will your Father in heaven give the Holy Spirit to those who ask him!"

Luke 11:5-13

Every good and perfect gift is from above, coming down from the Father of the heavenly lights, who does not change like shifting shadows.

James 1:17

He Provides Us a Heavenly Home

"In my Father's house are many rooms; if it were not so, I would have told you. I am going there to prepare a place for you. And if I go and prepare a place for you, I will come back and take you to be with me that you also may be where I am. You know the way to the place where I am going."

Thomas said to him, "Lord, we don't know where you are going, so how can we know the way?"

Jesus answered, "I am the way and the truth and the life. No one comes to the Father except through me. If you really knew me, you would know my Father as well. From now on, you do know him and have seen him."

John 14:2-7

FOR PERSONAL PRAYER:

Lord, I know You want me to turn over to You all my needs, desires, hopes, and dreams. Help me trust You more and more with every area of my life. Because You have graciously provided for me in the past, may I trust You completely for my future. Amen.

CHAPTER 9

'Suppose I'm a Single Parent?'

I t's not easy being a single parent," said Karen. "My day is crammed with survival activities: getting up early, getting Bobbie ready for nursery school, rushing off to work, coming home to household chores and child care for the evening. The next day it starts all over again.

"Perhaps the hardest part to get used to is the lack of support I sometimes feel, even from Christians at my church. After my husband died, some folks seemed to start avoiding me. I wish they would understand that I'm not looking for sympathy, just kindness."

FOR MEMORY:
In you, O LORD, I have taken refuge;
let me never be put to shame.

Psalm 71:1

FOR SILENT REFLECTION:

- *What beliefs carry me through the tough times?*

- *How can I use my trying circumstances for the best as I attempt effective parenting?*

- *What do I need most right now from Christian brothers and sisters? How can I let them know?*

- *What do I need most right now from God?*

Do You Feel Bitter about Past Hurts?

What misery is mine! I am like one who gathers summer fruit at the gleaning of the vineyard; there is no cluster of grapes to eat, none of the early figs that I crave.

Micah 7:1

Then Jesus told his disciples a parable to show them that they should always pray and not give up. He said: "In a certain town there was a judge who neither feared God nor cared about men. And there was a widow in that town who kept coming to him with the plea, 'Grant me justice against my adversary.' For some time he refused. But finally he said to himself, 'Even though I don't fear God or care about men, yet because this widow keeps bothering me, I will see that she gets justice, so that she won't eventually wear me out with her coming!" And the Lord said, "Listen to what the unjust judge says. And will not God bring about justice for his chosen ones, who cry out to him day and night? Will he keep putting them off?"

Luke 18:1-7

"In your anger do not sin": Do not let the sun go down while you are still angry.

Ephesians 4:26

157

Do You Feel Ashamed or Rejected?

I sought the LORD, and he answered me;
he delivered me from all my fears.
Those who look to him are radiant;
their faces are never covered with shame.

Psalm 34:4, 5

My disgrace is before me all day long,
and my face is covered with shame.

Psalm 44:15

You know how I am scorned,
disgraced and shamed; all my enemies are before you.

Psalm 69:19

In you, O LORD, I have taken refuge;
let me never be put to shame.

Psalm 71:1

Instead of their shame my people will receive a double portion,
and instead of disgrace they will rejoice in their inheritance;
and so they will inherit a double portion in their land,
and everlasting joy will be theirs.

Isaiah 61:7

You will have plenty to eat, until you are full,
and you will praise the name of the LORD your God,
who has worked wonders for you;
never again will my people be shamed.
Then you will know that I am in Israel,
that I am the LORD your God,
and that there is no other;
never again will my people be shamed.

Joel 2:26, 27

As it is written: "See, I lay in Zion a stone that causes
men to stumble and a rock that makes them fall, and
the one who trusts in him will never be put to
shame."

Romans 9:33

Do You Feel Discouraged?

My tears have been my food day and night,
while men say to me all day long, "Where is your
God?"

Psalm 42:3

Record my lament; list my tears on your scroll—
are they not in your record?

Psalm 56:8

The churning inside me never stops;

days of suffering confront me.

Job 30:27

I am feeble and utterly crushed;
I groan in anguish of heart.
All my longings lie open before you,
O Lord; my sighing is not hidden from you.
My heart pounds, my strength fails me;
even the light has gone from my eye.
My friends . . . avoid me because of my wounds;
my neighbors stay far away.

Psalm 38:8-11

For my days vanish like smoke;
my bones burn like glowing embers.
My heart is blighted and withered like grass;
I forget to eat my food.
Because of my loud groaning
I am reduced to skin and bones.
I am like a desert owl,
like an owl among the ruins.
I lie awake;
I have become like a bird alone on a roof.
All day long my enemies taunt me;
those who rail against me use my name as a curse.
For I eat ashes as my food
and mingle my drink with tears
because of your great wrath,

for you have taken me up and thrown me aside.
My days are like the evening shadow;
I wither away like grass.

Psalm 102:3-11

Hear my prayer, O LORD,
listen to my cry for help; be not deaf to my weeping.
For I dwell with you as an alien,
a stranger, as all my fathers were.

Psalm 39:12

God Comforts Those Who Cry

Those who sow in tears
will reap with songs of joy.

Psalm 126:5

This is what the LORD says: "Restrain your voice
from weeping and your eyes from tears, for your
work will be rewarded," declares the LORD.

Jeremiah 31:16a

I tell you the truth, you will weep and mourn while
the world rejoices. You will grieve, but your grief
will turn to joy. A woman giving birth to a child has
pain because her time has come; but when her baby
is born she forgets the anguish because of her joy
that a child is born into the world.

John 16:20, 21

161

During the days of Jesus' life on earth, he offered up prayers and petitions with loud cries and tears to the one who could save him from death, and he was heard because of his reverent submission.

Hebrews 5:7

And I heard a loud voice from the throne saying, "Now the dwelling of God is with men, and he will live with them. They will be his people, and God himself will be with them and be their God. He will wipe every tear from their eyes. There will be no more death or mourning or crying or pain, for the old order of things has passed away."

Revelation 21:3, 4

God Can Carry You Through Depression
But you, O God, do see trouble and grief;
you consider it to take it in hand.
The victim commits himself to you;
you are the helper of the fatherless.

Psalm 10:14

My flesh and my heart may fail,
but God is the strength of my heart and my portion forever.

Psalm 73:26

Unless the LORD had given me help,
I would soon have dwelt in the silence of death.
When I said, "My foot is slipping,"
your love, O LORD, supported me.
When anxiety was great within me,
your consolation brought joy to my soul.

Psalm 94:17-19

The Sovereign LORD has given me an instructed
tongue,
to know the word that sustains the weary.
He wakens me morning by morning,
wakens my ear to listen like one being taught.
The Sovereign LORD has opened my ears,
and I have not been rebellious;
I have not drawn back.
I offered my back to those who beat me,
my cheeks to those who pulled out my beard;
I did not hide my face from mocking and spitting.
Because the Sovereign LORD helps me,
I will not be disgraced. Therefore have I set my face
like flint,
and I know I will not be put to shame.
He who vindicates me is near.
Who then will bring charges against me?
Let us face each other! Who is my accuser?
Let him confront me!
It is the Sovereign LORD who helps me.

Who is he that will condemn me?
They will all wear out like a garment; the moths will
eat them up.
Who among you fears the LORD
and obeys the word of his servant?
Let him who walks in the dark, who has no light,
trust in the name of the LORD and rely on his God.

Isaiah 50:4-10

"Come to me, all you who are weary and burdened,
and I will give you rest. Take my yoke upon you and
learn from me, for I am gentle and humble in hearts,
and you will find rest for your souls. For my yoke is
easy and burden is light."

Matthew 11:28-30

"Do not let your hearts be troubled. Trust in God;
trust also in me. Peace I leave with you; my peace I
give you. I do not give to you as the world gives. Do
not let your hearts be troubled and do not be afraid."

John 14:1, 27

We are hard pressed on every side, but not crushed;
perplexed, but not in despair; persecuted, but not
abandoned; struck down, but not destroyed. Therefore we do not lose heart. . . . inwardly we are being
renewed day by day. For our light and momentary
troubles are achieving for us an eternal glory that far

outweighs them all. So we fix our eyes not on what is seen, but on what is unseen. For what is seen is temporary, but what is unseen is eternal.

II Corinthians 4:8, 9, 16-18

For the grace of God that brings salvation has appeared to all. . . . It teaches us to say "No" to ungodliness and worldly passions, and to live self-controlled, upright and godly lives in this present age, while we wait for the blessed hope—the glorious appearing of our great God and Savior, Jesus Christ, who gave himself for us to redeem us from all wickedness and to purify for himself a people that are his very own, eager to do what is good.

Titus 2:11-14

Do You Feel Guilty or Condemned?

God Accepts You

For we are God's workmanship, created in Christ Jesus to do good works, which God prepared in advance for us to do.

Ephesians 2:10

I remembered you, O God, and I groaned;
I mused, and my spirit grew faint.
You kept my eyes from closing;
I was too troubled to speak.

165

I thought about the former days,
the years of long ago;
I remembered my songs in the night.
My heart mused and my spirit inquired:
"Will the Lord reject forever?
Will he never show his favor again?
Has his unfailing love vanished forever?
Has his promise failed for all time?
Has God forgotten to be merciful?
Has he in anger withheld his compassion?"

Psalm 77:3-9

Zion said, "The LORD has forsaken me,
the Lord has forgotten me."
Can a mother forget the baby at her breast
and have no compassion on the child she has borne?
Though she may forget, I will not forget you!

Isaiah 49:14, 15

Who is a God like you,
who pardons sin and forgives the transgression
of the remnant of his inheritance?
You do not stay angry forever but delight to show mercy.
You will again have compassion on us;
you will trad our sins underfoot
and hurl all our iniquities into the depths of the sea.

Micah 7:18, 19

You Are Blameless in God's Eyes

Therefore, brothers, since we have confidence to enter the Most Holy Place by the blood of Jesus, by a new and living way opened for us through the curtain, that is, his body, and since we have a great priest over the house of God, let us draw near to God with a sincere heart in full assurance of faith, having our hearts sprinkled to cleanse us from a guilty conscience and having our bodies washed with pure water.

Hebrews 10:19-22

In this way, love is made complete among us so that we will have confidence on the day of judgment, because in this world we are like him. There is no fear in love. But perfect love drives out fear. . . .

I John 4:17, 18

FOR PERSONAL PRAYER:

Father, everything hasn't always worked out the way I've wanted it to. But You have never left me, no matter what. And You offer me a bright future at the dawn of every new day. Praise to You for accepting me through Your Son, Jesus. Amen.

The following titles are also available from Christian Parenting Books:

Bible Wisdom for Fathers
Bible Wisdom for Grandparents
Bible Wisdom for Mothers
Bible Wisdom for New Parents
Bible Wisdom for Newlyweds
Bible Wisdom for Parents
Bible Wisdom for Single Parents

BIBLE WISDOM FOR FATHERS

'What if I never had a good and loving father as a role model?'

'How can I build our home on a solid foundation of spiritual truth?'

'How can I handle my frustrations with the challenge of parenting?'

The expectations of a father have never been greater nor a father's role more important. But balancing the needs of marriage and children with the ever-increasing demands of a career often results in considerable stress. How does a father find balance and perspective?

Bible Wisdom for Fathers offers principles employed by successful fathers for generations—given by a heavenly Father who wants to help you be the best dad you can be.

BIBLE WISDOM FOR GRANDPARENTS

'How should I handle the opportunity I have to nurture my grandchildren?'

'Where can I turn for encouragement?'

'How can I face the future with hope?'

Grandparents are blessed with an incredible opportunity to nurture and inform a younger generation. Yet with the maturity and wisdom of life's later years often come discouragement and loss.

In *Bible Wisdom for Grandparents*, you'll discover ageless truths of strength, hope, and love that have been embraced by generations of people just like you.

BIBLE WISDOM FOR MOTHERS

'Where can I turn for the courage and
energy I need to be a good mom?'

'What if I've already made many mistakes parenting my kids?'

'How can I raise my child's self-esteem?'

The old saying "a mother's work is never done"
has never seemed more true. Meeting the children's needs while managing a household or
career can be overwhelming.

Bible Wisdom for Mothers helps to answer the
questions often asked by caring, concerned
moms by looking directly at the timeless wisdom of the Bible.

BIBLE WISDOM FOR NEW PARENTS

'How can we manage our own lives, handle the basics of child-rearing, and and still prepare our child for the future?'

'Where can we find help when we feel frustrated or inadequate?'

In today's world, new parents face an incredible challenge. Juggling the demands of everyday home life and careers can lead to feelings of frustration, anxiety and guilt.

In *Bible Wisdom for New Parents*, you and your spouse will discover answers to your deepest concerns—and guidance that has stood the test of time. You will find a God who understands the pains and pleasures of parenthood and can help you face your new responsibilities with confidence.

BIBLE WISDOM FOR NEWLYWEDS

'What does it really mean to be committed to one another?'

'What are the joys and challenges of our new roles?'

'How can we handle disappointment or disillusionment during our first years together?'

Successful marriage has never been easy. But today's pressures and faster pace mean an extra dose of commitment and understanding is needed for couples facing such contemporary concerns as career choices, finances, family relationships, and intimacy.

In *Bible Wisdom for Newlyweds*, you will find insight to strengthen and deepen your relationship—with your spouse and with God.

BIBLE WISDOM FOR PARENTS

'What lasting values can we pass on to our children?'

'How can we cope when we feel frustrated with our parenting responsibilities?'

'How might we best love our kids and do what's best for them?'

Raising kids in today's fast-paced, stress-filled world is an awesome responsibility. And just when you're getting a handle on it, everything seems to change—a child's needs, society's values, the demands of your own life.

In *Bible Wisdom for Parents*, you'll discover words of encouragement, comfort, strength, and love that have satisfied successful parents for centuries.

BIBLE WISDOM FOR SINGLE PARENTS

'What steps can I take to raise my children in
the best way possible?'

'How can I cope when I'm feeling lonely?'

'How can I focus on God's goodness rather than
on my own problems?'

Raising kids can be a daunting challenge when
you have to do it alone. With little or no help,
single parents must meet their children's needs
and manage a career at the same time.

Bible Wisdom for Single Parents offers time-
tested truths that have encouraged and
strengthened many single parents. You can find
in its pages a heavenly Father who wants to
meet your needs and help you lovingly raise
your kids.